Houseplants

A practical guide to their selection and care

Su Whale NDSF FBFA

Guzmania lingulata

Jago
PUBLISHING LIMITED

Published by:

Jago Publishing Ltd.
23 Tomlan Road
West Heath
Birmingham
B31 3NX

info@jagopublishing.co.uk
www.jagopublishing.co.uk

First Published 2019

Text copyright © Su Whale NDSF FBFA 2019

The author reserves all rights.

The author and publisher have made every effort to ensure the accuracy of the information contained in this book at the time of going to press. They cannot however be held responsible for any loss or inconvenience resulting from the use of information contained in this book. They also cannot be held responsible for omissions or errors that may occur due to changes in commercial availability or botanical re-classification.

A CIP catalogue record for this book is available from the British Library.

ISBN 978-0-9568713-4-3

All rights reserved. No part of this publication may be reproduced, stored in any retrieval system or transmitted in any form or by any means, electronic, mechanical, photocopying, recording or otherwise without the prior permission of the publishers.

Designed by Corner House Design and Print Ltd, Manchester.

Printed in England by Coloprint Ltd, Birmingham.

Cover Image ©Olga P. Shutterstock.com

Contents

Introduction – Why have a houseplant? **4**

Houseplant Care Basics **5**

How to use this book **6 & 7**

Botanical List from A to Z **8–132**

Bromeliads & Cacti **133**

Ferns & Orchids **134**

Palms & Succulents **135**

Caring for Planted Designs **136**

Composts & Repotting **137**

Pests & Diseases **138 & 139**

Glossary **140 & 141**

Index **142 & 143**

Acknowledgements & thanks **144**

Sansevieria cylindrica

Introduction

Having spent over thirty years working in the cut flower and pot plant industry, I have discovered that there are generally only two questions customers ask when purchasing a houseplant. First is, 'where can I put it?' the second, 'how often should I water it?' If you are that person and are looking for a straightforward, practical guide to houseplant care which will provide you with the answers to those questions, (and much more besides!) then this book is for you.

Why have a houseplant?

There are so many reasons to fill your home or business with houseplants. They are stylish and interesting, and come in so many different shapes, sizes and colours; some flowering, some prickly, some just luscious green, that it's guaranteed that there will be at least one, if not more, to suit any décor and aspect.

Houseplants are good for your health as well. NASA's study to research ways to clean the air in space stations found that not only were plants able to do their normal, fantastic, job of photosynthesis in space (removing carbon dioxide from the air to replace it with oxygen) but many common houseplants also provided a natural and effective way of removing a wide range of toxins from the air.

How to choose your houseplant

Preliminary research into what sort of plant would be right for you and your home should always be the first step, as there is no point purchasing a difficult plant if you haven't the time to give it the care and attention it needs. Neither do you want to buy something which will eventually grow to the size of a small tree if you live in a flat.

What often tends to happen though is that you are either given a houseplant or you are seduced by one in a garden centre or florists and before you know it, it's come home with you.

We've all done it.

If this is the case, then place your new addition in an 'average' spot, not too hot or cold, not too shady or sunny to give it time to acclimatise to the change in its environment. Avoid moving it until, by using this book for your research, you have been able to find just the right spot for it so that you and your houseplant can develop a long-lasting and mutually thriving relationship.

Let's hear it for the houseplant!

Houseplant Care Basics

Some General Do's and Don'ts

Temperature:
Do avoid extremes; neither scorching sun though glass in summer or a draughty cold windowsill behind curtains in winter will do your houseplant any good. An average room temperature of 18–21°C/65–70°F will keep most plants happy. Try not to subject your plant to sudden changes in temperature either.

Watering:
Don't let your plant sit swimming in water, and if it's in a pot cover, check it regularly. Don't let it dry out completely either, if anything, err on the side of underwatering rather than overwatering.

Use tepid water or rainwater whenever possible and if watering from above, make sure that the water is reaching the compost, not running off the leaves. As a general rule, allow compost to dry out slightly in between watering.

Humidity:
Many houseplants originate from warm, tropical areas so require a humid atmosphere, particularly if they are in a centrally heated room. Create humidity by using a spray bottle filled with tepid water, misting the leaves and air around the plant. If your plant requires high humidity, stand it on top of a saucer of water filled with pebbles or gravel which should be refreshed every few weeks to stop it from becoming stagnant. Grouping plants together also helps to build and maintain humidity. When misting plants avoid wetting flowers or hairy leaves as this can encourage mould.

Light:
Most plants will thrive in bright, indirect light, i.e. fully exposed to light, but not in direct sun, such as an east or north facing windowsill. No houseplant will grow in the total dark.

For even growth, turn plants occasionally and never let leaves touch windows in hot summers.

Feeding:
Regular watering flushes away natural nutrients in compost so do feed your plants, especially in spring and summer when most houseplants are in their growing period. Houseplant food is available from most garden centres and homeware shops. There are also specialist feeds available for cacti and orchids.

Compost:
General multi-purpose houseplant compost is ideal for most houseplants, plus there are specialist composts for orchids, bulbs and cacti. For more information on composts and repotting see page 137.

Winter Care:
Many houseplants benefit from a period of winter rest, roughly between November and February. It gives them a chance to recuperate and recharge their batteries. During this time, reduce watering, stop feeding and place the plant in a cooler spot if possible, such as an unheated, frost free room.

How to use this book

Each page is laid out in the same order for easy reference.

Botanical Name: Houseplants are listed in alphabetical order of botanical names; there is an index of common names on pages 142 & 143.

Common Name: Some of the plants popular but non-scientific names.

Plant Notes: A guide to pronunciation and a brief description of the general characteristics of the plant, relevant to it being grown specifically for indoors, not as it may be found in the wild or in a garden.

Type: Whether a Bromeliad, Cactus, Fern, Foliage houseplant, Flowering houseplant, Orchid, Palm or Succulent.

More information about these plant types can be found on pages 133 to 135.

Height: Mini – up to 15cm/6". Small – up to 30cm/12".
Medium – up to 60cm/24". Tall – 90cm/36" upwards.

These are approximate to be used as a guide only. Bear in mind that environmental conditions will affect the height and spread of a plant.

Colour: Foliage colour on a green houseplant, flower colour on flowering plants.

Ideal Spot: To help you find the perfect place for your plant.

Skill Level: Some plants take more looking after than others. I have divided them broadly into three groups;

Easy. Unfussy plant, good for beginners.
Average. Will need some attention to get the best results.
Expert. A plant you will need to be prepared to put some work into.

Longevity: Something for the summer or a plant for life? An approximate indication to the plants lifespan when kept in ideal conditions.

Essential Care: The plants basic care requirements.

Temperature: Cool (an unheated room indoors) 10–13°C/50–55°F.
Warm (average room temperature) 13–18°C/55–65°F.
Hot (conservatory in summer) 18–27°C/65–80°F.

These temperature guides are for when the plant is in its growing/flowering stage which is generally spring through to autumn.

Watering: Requirements when in growing/flowering period. As a general rule always allow the compost to dry out slightly in between watering.

Humidity: Low – plant requires little or no extra humidity.
Medium – Mist every 3 to 4 days with tepid water.
High – Use pebble tray as well as frequent misting.

How to use this book

Light: The optimum light level for your plant, remember that light levels change throughout the day and over the seasons.

Feeding: Plants in pots need to be fed to replenish essential nutrients in the compost. A houseplant all-purpose liquid fertilizer is adequate for the majority of green and flowering houseplants. There are specialist feeds available for orchids, cacti and carnivorous plants. Always follow the manufacturers recommendations for dilution.

General Care: Further advice on caring for your houseplant. This includes:
Seasonality and/or flowering period.
Whether or not the plant can go outside in summer.
General plant maintenance.

Troubleshooting: Most common problems and their most likely cause which is generally down to not giving the plant the ideal growing conditions it requires. This list is not exhaustive!

Pests & Diseases: Those which the plant may be most prone to. Prevention is always better than cure when it comes to dealing with unwanted pests, so check your plant regularly. A list of the most common pests and diseases and how to deal with them can be found on pages 138 & 139.

In a separate box:
Further information specifically relevant to the houseplant, including:
Propagation: When propagation is something that can be undertaken by the enthusiast rather than the professional.
Uses in Design Work: Suggestions on how some houseplants can be used in floristry and flower arranging.
Winter care: For some plants winter rest is essential for their wellbeing.

In a separate box:
Botanical information:
Family
Genus
Origin

Symbols:

 Suitable for use in floristry. Either all, or parts of the plant can be used in design work.

 Poisonous/toxic. Some houseplants are harmless to humans but toxic to pets. Always keep plants out of reach of curious children and animals. Wash hands after handling or wear gloves.

 Plant has sharp spines, points or serrated edges or has sap or hairs that can be an irritant.

 Some plants have been singled out by NASA as having excellent air purifying qualities.

Abutilon

Common Name: **Flowering maple, Chinese maple**

Plant Notes:	Pronounced 'a-BEW-til-lon'. A vigorous shrub with attractive lobed leaves, sometimes variegated. It bears pendulous, colourful bell-shaped flowers.
Type:	Flowering shrub.
Colour:	Yellow, orange and deep pink flowers.
Ideal Spot:	Conservatory, sheltered patio in summer.
Height:	Tall. 90cm/36".
Skill Level:	Easy.
Longevity:	5–10 years.

Essential Care:
- **Temperature:** Warm. 18–24°C/65–75°F.
- **Watering:** Keep compost moist spring to autumn, water sparingly in winter.
- **Humidity:** Low. Mist occasionally in warm weather.
- **Light:** Bright, indirect sunlight.
- **Feeding:** Every two weeks, spring to autumn.

General Care:
- Flowering period; spring to autumn.
- Some varieties are suitable for hanging baskets.
- Can go outside in summer.

Troubleshooting:
- If shedding leaves, air temperature is too cold.

Pests & Diseases:
- When kept indoors, can be susceptible to red spider mite, mealy bugs and scale insects.

After Flowering:
Prune lightly in autumn cutting away any damaged or wayward stems using secateurs. Overwinter in a cool, frost free spot. To keep it bushy, trim again in spring by approximately one third.

Family: Malvaceae.
Genus: Abutilon.
Origin: Tropical regions.

Abutilon x hybridum

Adiantum

Common Name: Maidenhair fern, Delta maidenhair

Plant Notes: Pronounced 'add-e-AN-tum'. A delicate plant with arching wiry stems supporting small triangular leaflets. Often seen growing between rocks around waterfalls and other water outlets.

Type: Fern.
Colour: Fresh, bright green with black stems.
Ideal Spot: Bathroom or kitchen.
Height: Small/medium. 38cm/15".
Skill Level: Average.
Longevity: 5 + years.

Essential Care:
- **Temperature:** Warm. 13–18°C/55–65°F.
- **Watering:** Keep compost moist, but not wet. Reduce watering in winter.
- **Humidity:** High. Mist weekly with tepid water, stand in pebble tray.
- **Light:** Indirect, will tolerate light shade.
- **Feeding:** Every two weeks spring to autumn.

General Care:
- They dislike dry air; high humidity is essential.
- Avoid sudden changes in temperature and direct heat sources.
- Minimum winter temperature of 10°C/50°F.

Troubleshooting:
- Yellow leaf tips are a sign of overwatering.
- Fronds drying up; not enough humidity.

Pests & Diseases:
- Scale insects and mealy bugs.

Trivia:
Its common name comes from the dark, shiny leafstalks which are said to resemble human hair.

Family: Pteridaceae.
Genus: Adiantum.
Origin: Tropical & subtropical regions.

Adiantum raddianum

Aechmea

Common Name: **Silver vase plant**

Plant Notes: Pronounced 'EKK-me-uh'. An impressive plant with strap-like, serrated silvery-grey leaves. It produces a colourful bract from its central rosette which will flower from early summer to autumn.

Type: Bromeliad.
Colour: Green/grey with pink and lilac flower.
Ideal Spot: Sitting room, porch, conservatory.

Height: Medium. 60cm/24".
Skill Level: Easy.
Longevity: 3–4 years.

Essential Care:
- **Temperature:** Warm/hot. 15–21°C/60–70°F.
- **Watering:** Soft or distilled water into central leaf well. Refresh every 3–4 weeks.
- **Humidity:** Low. Mist weekly in hot weather.
- **Light:** Bright, but not full sun.
- **Feeding:** Every two weeks when in flower.

General Care:
- Winter minimum temperature of 15°C/60°F.
- Dislikes sudden changes in temperature.
- Can become top heavy once in flower.
- The parent plant will flower only once.

Troubleshooting:
- Brown tips on leaves; too hot and dry.
- Bract discolouration; too cold.

Pests & Diseases:
- Scale insects and mealy bugs.

After Flowering:
Once the flower has died, cut it away. The parent plant will also eventually die, but will produce offsets which can be carefully removed and re-potted. See page 133.

Family: Bromeliaceae.
Genus: Aechmea.
Origin: Brazil.

Aechmea fasciata

Aeonium

Common Name: **Pin wheel, Houseleek**

Plant Notes: Both decorative and dramatic, this varied group is characterised by woody stems and tight rosettes of fleshy leaves from which small, star-shaped flowers emerge from spring to autumn on mature plants.

Type: Succulent.
Colour: Mid to bright green, burgundy.
Ideal Spot: Unheated porches or conservatories.
Height: Small to tall. 30–90cm/12–36".
Skill Level: Easy.
Longevity: 10 + years.

Essential Care:
- **Temperature:** Warm. Daytime, 18°C/65°F. Night, cool. 10°C/50°F.
- **Watering:** Generously in summer but avoid waterlogging.
- **Humidity:** Low. Fresh air is more important.
- **Light:** South or west facing, protect from direct sunlight.
- **Feeding:** Every two weeks during summer.

General Care:
- Can be placed outside in summer.
- Burgundy varieties will turn green if in too shady a spot.
- Some species become dormant in very hot summers.

Troubleshooting:
- Leaf curl is caused by hot, direct sunlight.
- Prone to root rot if overwatered, use cactus compost.

Pests & Diseases:
- Aphids and mealy bugs.

Winter Care:
Not frost hardy, overwinter indoors. Reduce watering, just keeping compost moist and feed monthly to encourage spring flowering. Move outside in spring once frosts are over.

Family: Aeonium.
Genus: Crassulaceae.
Origin: East Africa & Canary Islands.

Aeonium 'Zwartkop'

Agave

Common Name: American century plant, Agave

Plant Notes: Pronounced 'A-GAR-ve'. A tough desert plant with toothed, fleshy leaves that grow in a distinctive rosette shape. Easy to care for, choose one of the smaller growing varieties for the home.

Type: Succulent.
Colour: Green/blue, some with cream margins.
Ideal Spot: Conservatory, porch or patio.
Height: Mini to tall. 15–90cm/6–36".
Skill Level: Easy.
Longevity: 10 + years.

Essential Care:
- **Temperature:** Cool/hot. 10–30°C/50–86°F.
- **Watering:** Once a month in summer, sparingly in winter.
- **Humidity:** Low. Misting not necessary, but they do appreciate fresh air.
- **Light:** Bright, south facing sunny position.
- **Feeding:** Every two weeks spring to autumn.

General Care:
- Can go outside in summer in light shade.
- Water sparingly in winter.
- Agave can withstand a certain amount of neglect.
- Sap can be an irritant.

Troubleshooting:
- Base rot is caused by overwatering.

Pests & Diseases:
- Prone to scale insects on young growth.

Trivia:
Agave syrup is a natural sweetener obtained from several species of the plant and can be used as a substitute for sugar and honey.

Family: Asparagaceae.
Genus: Agave.
Origin: Tropical South America, Southern & Western United States.

Agave spp.

Aglaonema

Common Name: Chinese evergreen, Silver evergreen

Plant Notes: Pronounced 'Ag-lay-oh-NEMA'. A popular, slow growing plant with attractively marked leaves, many with distinctive variegation. Small insignificant flowers are followed by red berries.

CO_2 ✗

Type: Foliage houseplant.
Colour: Bright green with cream/silver markings.
Ideal Spot: Any room shaded from direct sunlight.
Height: Medium. 60cm/24".
Skill Level: Average.
Longevity: 3 + years.

Essential Care:

- **Temperature:** Warm/hot. 18–24°C/65–75°F.
- **Watering:** Thoroughly in summer, sparingly in winter.
- **Humidity:** High. Mist weekly; it thrives in a moist, warm atmosphere.
- **Light:** Semi-shade for green leaved varieties, brighter for variegated but out of direct sun.
- **Feeding:** Every two weeks spring to autumn.

General Care:

- Allow compost to dry out slightly between watering.
- Don't prune leaves back, this will kill the plant.
- Suitable to go outside in summer in a sheltered position.

Troubleshooting:

- Yellow patches on leaves is a sign that air is too cold or too dry.

Pests & Diseases:

- Mealy bugs and botrytis.

Trivia:
Aglaonema have the ability to remove toxins from the air. They are in NASA's top 15 of clean air plants.

Family: Araceae.
Genus: Aglaonema.
Origin: South-East America.

Aglaonema Snow White

Alocasia

Common Name: **Elephant's ear**

Plant Notes: Pronounced 'Al-o-KAY-see-uh'. An impressive houseplant with large, boldly marked leaves. Only truly happy in a hot, humid environment.
Type: Foliage houseplant.
Colour: Dark green, cream/white veins.
Ideal Spot: Conservatory or greenhouse.
Height: Medium. 60cm/24".
Skill Level: Expert.
Longevity: 5 + years.

Essential Care:
- **Temperature:** Warm/hot. 18–25°C/65–77°F.
- **Watering:** Keep compost moist using rainwater or distilled water.
- **Humidity:** High. Mist daily, use a pebble tray.
- **Light:** Semi-shade in summer, bright light in winter.
- **Feeding:** Every two weeks, spring to autumn.

General Care:
- Winter minimum temperature of 15°C/60°F.
- In winter stop feeding and reduce watering.
- Clean leaves regularly with a damp cloth.

Troubleshooting:
- Discoloured leaves indicate over exposure to sunlight.

Pests & Diseases:
- Can be prone to red spider mite in a warm, dry atmosphere.

Trivia:
A. macrorrhizos or 'Giant Taro' has leaves that can grow up to 1m/39" in length. In the Philippines the leaf stalks are chewed to relieve toothache.

Family: Araceae.
Genus: Alocasia.
Origin: Tropical Asia.

Alocasia x amazonica

Aloe

Common Name: **Aloe**

Plant Notes: Pronounced 'Al-low'. A varied group of plants, notable for their compact rosettes of spear shaped leaves many with marked variegation. They produce tall, impressive flower spikes.

CO_2

Type: Succulent.
Colour: Green, blue/green.
Ideal Spot: Sunny windowsill.
Height: Mini/small. 15–30cm/6–12".
Skill Level: Easy.
Longevity: 10 + years.

Essential Care:
- **Temperature:** Cool/hot. 5–30°C/41–86°F.
- **Watering:** Every two weeks in summer.
- **Humidity:** Low. Misting not necessary but they appreciate fresh air.
- **Light:** Sunny but with protection from direct sun in summer.
- **Feeding:** Monthly in summer using diluted cactus feed.

General Care:
- Undemanding and tough, Aloe can thrive on a certain amount of neglect.
- Often have spiny or serrated edges, handle with care.
- Avoid water sitting in centre of rosette.

Troubleshooting:
- Soft, wilting leaves are a sign of overwatering.

Pests & Diseases:
- Aloe is not particularly prone to pests and diseases.

Winter Care:
Not frost hardy so overwinter indoors. Reduce watering to a minimum and stop feeding. Keeping it at a lower temperature of 5–10°C/41–50°F, will help to encourage the plant to flower.

Family: Asphodelaceae.
Genus: Aloe.
Origin: Arabia.

Aloe chinensis

Ananas

Common Name: **Ornamental pineapple**

Plant Notes: Pronounced 'a-NAN-ass'. A decorative plant with plain or striped leaves edged with sharp spines. Under the right conditions it can produce small, generally inedible, fruits.

Type: Bromeliad.
Colour: Dark green, some striped pink/cream.
Ideal Spot: Warm, sunny room.
Height: Medium. 60cm/24".
Skill Level: Easy.
Longevity: 5 + years.

Essential Care:
- **Temperature:** Warm/hot. 15–21°C/60–70°F.
- **Watering:** Keep compost moist but not wet using rainwater if possible.
- **Humidity:** Medium. Mist every 2 to 3 days with tepid water.
- **Light:** Happy in bright sunshine.
- **Feeding:** Add liquid fertilizer every 2 to 3 weeks when misting.

General Care:
- Needs a winter minimum of 15°C/60°F.
- In winter when plant is resting, reduce watering and stop feeding.

Troubleshooting:
- Brown tips on leaves; air is too dry.

Pests & Diseases:
- Can be troubled by scale insects.

Trivia:
The Dunmore Pineapple is a hothouse in the shape of a pineapple built by John Murray, 4th Earl of Dunmore in 1761. Its purpose? To grow pineapples, naturally.

Family: Bromeliaceae.
Genus: Ananas.
Origin: Central & South America.

Ananas comosus

Anthurium

Common Name: Flamingo flower, Tail flower

Plant Notes: Pronounced 'Ann-THUR-re-am'. A tropical flowering plant with decorative heart shaped leaves that produce striking, long-lasting flowers.

Type: Flowering houseplant.
Colour: Glossy green; red, white, peach, pink flowers.
Ideal Spot: Sunny conservatory or porch.
Height: Tall. 90m/36".
Skill Level: Average.
Longevity: 5 + years.

Essential Care:

- **Temperature range:** Warm/hot. 18–21°C/65–70°F.
- **Watering:** Little but often, always keep compost moist.
- **Humidity:** High. Mist daily and stand in pebble tray.
- **Light:** Not full sun but will need bright light for it to flower.
- **Feeding:** In summer only, once every two weeks.

General Care:

- Very sensitive to changes in temperature and humidity.
- Requires minimum of 15°C/60°F in winter.
- Any roots seen above surface should be gently pushed under the soil.

Troubleshooting:

- Yellowing leaves; either too cold, dry or wet.

Pests & Diseases:

- Mealy bugs, red spider mite and aphids.

Flowering:
Although relatively easy to keep as a foliage plant; a minimum temperature of 21°C/70°F and constant high humidity is required if they are to produce flowers successfully.

Family: Araceae.
Genus: Anthurium.
Origin: Central & South America.

Anthurium andraeanum

Aphelandra

Common Name: **Zebra plant, Saffron spike**

Plant Notes: Pronounced 'AFF-a-land-dra'. A tropical plant with glossy foliage and distinctive veining on its leaves. Produces angular flower spikes which can last for up to eight weeks.

Type: Flowering/foliage houseplant.
Colour: Deep green with silver veining, yellow flower.
Ideal Spot: Warm conservatory or bathroom.
Height: Medium. 60cm/24".
Skill Level: Expert.
Longevity: 3 + years.

Essential Care:
- **Temperature:** Warm/hot. 18–21°C/65–70°F.
- **Watering:** Freely in summer, keep moist in winter.
- **Humidity:** High. Mist daily in summer with tepid water.
- **Light:** Bright spot out of direct sun.
- **Feeding:** Every two weeks from spring to autumn.

General Care:
- Summer flowering.
- Winter temperature no less than 12°C/50°F.
- Very susceptible to changes in temperature and draughts.

Troubleshooting:
- Cool air, direct sun or draughts will cause leaf drop.
- Leaves will scorch if exposed to direct sunlight.

Pests & Diseases:
- Aphids, mealy bugs; botrytis if overwatered.

After Flowering:
Remove faded flower bracts and cut back to a single pair of leaves. Rest in a cool spot, reduce watering and stop feeding. Resume normal care in spring.

Family: Acanthaceae.
Genus: Aphelandra.
Origin: Tropical America.

Aphelandra squarrosa

Asparagus

Common Name: **Emerald fern**

Plant Notes: Pronounced 'Asp-SPARA-gus'. A bushy, slightly untidy plant with a trailing habit that makes it an ideal candidate for hanging baskets. It bears small white insignificant flowers.

Type: Foliage houseplant.
Colour: Emerald green.
Ideal Spot: A warm, but not hot, room.
Height: Medium. 60cm/24".
Skill Level: Easy.
Longevity: 5 + years.

Essential Care:
- **Temperature:** Warm. 10–15°C/50–60°F.
- **Watering:** Water regularly spring to autumn, more sparingly in winter.
- **Humidity:** Medium. Mist weekly, especially in heated rooms.
- **Light:** Semi-shade to bright light, protect from direct sunlight.
- **Feeding:** Monthly in spring and summer.

General Care:
- Will not tolerate a constant high temperature.
- Mist in winter if in a centrally heated room.
- Can be cut back if too large or showing signs of yellowing.

Troubleshooting:
- Leaf drop and yellowing foliage, too dry and/or room is too hot.

Pests & Diseases:
- Not especially troubled by pests and diseases.

> **Trivia:**
> Although not a true fern, it has been commonly called so since Victorian times, when it was a popular indoor plant for jardinières.

> **Family:** Asparagaceae.
> **Genus:** Asparagus.
> **Origin:** South Africa.

A. densiflorus 'Sprengeri'

Asparagus

Common Name: **Plume asparagus, Foxtail fern**

Plant Notes: Pronounced 'Asp-SPARA-gus'. A delicate looking plant with feathery arching plumes of tiny needle-like leaves. It bears small white flowers followed by bright red berries.

Type: Foliage houseplant.
Colour: Bright green.
Ideal Spot: A warm room, away from direct heat.
Height: Medium. 60cm/24".
Skill Level: Easy.
Longevity: 5 + years.

Essential Care:
- **Temperature:** Warm/hot. 13–24°C/55–75°F.
- **Watering:** Water regularly spring to autumn, more sparingly in winter.
- **Humidity:** Medium. Mist occasionally, especially in heated rooms.
- **Light:** Semi-shade to bright light, protect from direct sunlight.
- **Feeding:** Monthly in spring and summer.

General Care:
- Mist occasionally in winter if in a centrally heated room.
- Has hidden thorns, handle with care.

Troubleshooting:
- Leaf drop and yellowing foliage; compost is too dry and/or room is too hot.

Pests & Diseases:
- Not especially troubled by pests and diseases.

A. densiflorus 'Myersii'

Trivia:
The edible *A. officinalis* has been cultivated for thousands of years; asparagus means 'shoot' or 'spear' and 'officinalis' of the dispensary – referring to its medicinal qualities.

Family: Asparagaceae.
Genus: Asparagus.
Origin: South Africa.

Aspidistra

Common Name: **Cast iron plant**

Plant Notes: Pronounced 'Asp-SPID-dis-tra'. A trusty stalwart, with robust foliage popular for flower arranging. As its name suggests, regarded as being virtually indestructible.

Type: Foliage houseplant.
Colour: Dark green; pale cream variegation.
Ideal Spot: Prefers cool, shady areas.

Height: Tall. 90cm/36".
Skill Level: Easy.
Longevity: 15 + years.

Essential Care:
- **Temperature:** Cool. 7–13°C/45–55°F.
- **Watering:** Regularly spring to autumn, let compost dry out slightly in-between.
- **Humidity:** Low. Sponge leaves occasionally.
- **Light:** Will tolerate some shade, protect from direct sunlight.
- **Feeding:** Monthly in spring and summer.

General Care:
- Minimum winter temperature 7°C/45°F.
- Reduce watering in winter.
- Slow growing, its biggest enemy is dust!
- One of the few plants that can deal with poor light.

Troubleshooting:
- A wilting plant indicates saturated compost, be careful to not overwater.

Pests & Diseases:
- Scale insects, red spider mite, mealy bugs.

> **Trivia:**
> Aspidistras do flower; however they are inconspicuous, appearing singly, poking out at soil level. They grow this way as they are pollinated by slugs and snails.

Family: Asparagaceae.
Genus: Aspidistra.
Origin: Far East.

Aspidistra elatior

Asplenium

Common Name: Bird's nest fern, Spleenwort

Plant Notes: Pronounced 'asp-SPLEE-knee-um'. An impressive fern with glossy, undivided fronds. An epiphyte in its natural habitat, it is fast growing and easy to care for.

Type: Fern.
Colour: Bright green.
Ideal Spot: Any warm, bright room.
Height: Medium. 60cm/24".
Skill Level: Easy.
Longevity: 3 + years.

Essential Care:
- **Temperature:** Warm/hot. 15–24°C/60–75°F.
- **Watering:** Keep moist, do not allow compost to dry out.
- **Humidity:** High. Mist every 2 to 3 days with tepid water.
- **Light:** A shady spot with indirect sunlight.
- **Feeding:** Every two weeks during spring and summer.

General Care:
- Try not to handle young, growing fronds.
- Stand in pebble tray to increase humidity.
- Reduce watering in winter.
- Dislikes direct heat sources and draughts.

Troubleshooting:
- Yellow leaf tips are a sign of overwatering.

Pests & Diseases:
- Susceptible to scale insects.

> **Trivia:**
> The name "spleenwort" is from the old belief that, because of the shape of its leaves it was useful for ailments of the spleen. Wort is an ancient English word that simply means plant.

Family: Aspleniaceae.
Genus: Asplenium.
Origin: Tropical regions.

Asplenium nidus

Begonia (flowering)

Common Name: **Begonia**

Plant Notes: Pronounced 'BE-go-knee-uh.' One of the most popular flowering pot plants on the market. Available in a wild range of colours, they are bright, cheerful and reliable.

Type: Flowering houseplant.
Colour: All except blue, green and purple.
Ideal Spot: Any bright, warm room.
Height: Mini/small. 30cm/12".
Skill Level: Easy.
Longevity: Flowers approx. 3 months.

Essential Care:
- **Temperature:** Warm. 15–21°C/60–70°F.
- **Watering:** Keep compost moist but not waterlogged.
- **Humidity:** Medium. Mist air around plant weekly.
- **Light:** Bright, sunny spot but shade from direct summer sun.
- **Feeding:** Once a week while in flower.

General Care:
- Begonia's natural flowering period is in the winter.
- Don't allow compost to dry out and deadhead regularly.
- Don't turn pots, this can cause bud drop.
- Once it has finished flowering discard or recycle.

Troubleshooting:
- Plant collapse or rotting leaves; overwatering.
- Brown tips on leaves/yellow leaves; too dry/dark.
- Bud drop; over exposure to ethylene gas.

Pests & Diseases:
- Botrytis and powdery mildew, also aphids and red spider mite.

Trivia:
Begonia 'Kimjongilia' has bright red double flowers and was named after the late leader of North Korea, Kim Jong-Il.

Family: Begoniaceae.
Genus: Begonia.
Origin: Brazil.

Begonia elatior

Begonia (foliage)

Common Name: **Painted leaf Begonia**

Plant Notes: Pronounced 'BE-go-knee-uh.' Very decorative plants grown primarily for their exotic, strikingly marked asymmetrical leaves. Compact and low growing, they are popular as a summer bedding plant.

Type: Foliage houseplant.
Colour: Silver, green, red, burgundy, brown.
Ideal Spot: Any bright, warm room.
Height: Mini/small 30cm/12".
Skill Level: Easy.
Longevity: 1–2 years.

Essential Care:
- **Temperature:** Warm. 15–21°C/60–70°F.
- **Watering:** Keep compost moist, reduce watering in winter.
- **Humidity:** Medium. Mist air around plants weekly, avoiding the leaves.
- **Light:** Bright, sunny spot but shade from direct summer sun.
- **Feeding:** Every two weeks spring to autumn.

General Care:
- Don't let the plant stand in water.
- They appreciate good air circulation.
- Tiny hairs on the stems can be an irritant, wear gloves if necessary.

Troubleshooting:
- Rotting stems; compost is too wet.
- Brown tips on leaves; air is too dry.

Pests & Diseases:
- Botrytis and powdery mildew, also aphids and red spider mite.

> **Trivia:**
> There are estimated to be around 2,000 Begonia hybrids, many of which can be attributed to Dutch growers who started mass production after WWII.

Family: Begoniaceae.
Genus: Begonia.
Origin: Tropical regions.

Begonia rex.

Bougainvillea

Common Name: Paper plant, Paper flower

Plant Notes: Pronounced 'Bore-gan-VIL-e-are'. Native to tropical countries where the dazzling colours of this vigorous flowering climber can be admired in their full glory.

Type: Flowering climber.
Colour: Pink/purple, coral, white, yellow.
Ideal Spot: Sunny conservatory or porch.
Height: Tall. 90cm/36".
Skill Level: Expert.
Longevity: 3–5 years.

Essential Care:
- **Temperature:** Warm. 15–21°C/60–70°F.
- **Watering:** By immersion, allow to dry out slightly in between.
- **Humidity:** Medium. Spray weekly with tepid water.
- **Light:** Full sun during flowering period. Can go outside in summer.
- **Feeding:** Once a week February to October.

General Care:
- Flowering period April to August.
- Prune lightly after each flush of flowers.
- Keeping it in a pot will restrict its growth.
- It will naturally lose some of its leaves in winter.

Troubleshooting:
- No flowers, needs more light; 5 to 6 hours a day.
- Leaf drop in summer; too dry.
- Yellow leaves; overwatering.

Pests & Diseases:
- Red spider mite, mealy bugs.

Winter Care:
Place in a cool, frost free spot, minimum temperature of 7°C/45°F. Stop feeding and water sparingly. Prune back lightly in February and resume normal watering and feeding once new buds appear.

Family: Nyctaginaceae.
Genus: Bougainvillea.
Origin: Tropical South America.

Bougainvillea 'Alexandra'

Buxus

Common Name: **Common box**

Plant Notes: Pronounced 'Bucks-us.' An evergreen slow growing shrub with glossy green leathery leaves. Dense in habit it will provide a background for more exotic plants and add shape and visual weight to houseplant collections.

Type: Shrub.
Colour: Dark green.
Ideal Spot: Cool, but brightly lit.
Height: Medium. 60cm/24".
Skill Level: Easy.
Longevity: 10 + years.

Essential Care:
- **Temperature:** Cool/warm. 10–18°C/50–65°F.
- **Watering:** Water well but allow compost to dry out slightly in between.
- **Humidity:** Low. Mist occasionally in warm weather.
- **Light:** Bright or semi-shade, will tolerate some direct sun.
- **Feeding:** Every two weeks spring to autumn.

General Care:
- Can go outside in summer.
- Ideal candidate for topiary.
- Pinch out growing tips to keep it bushy.
- Prune mid to late spring to keep it in shape.

Troubleshooting:
- Brown leaves; sun or wind scorch.
- Leaf drop; compost is too dry.

Pests & Diseases:
- Box blight, red spider mite.

Winter Care:
Reduce watering and stop feeding. Buxus are fully hardy but if overwintering inside, move to a cool spot and water just enough to stop the root ball from drying out.

Family: Buxaceae.
Genus: Buxus.
Origin: S/W Europe & North Africa.

Buxus sempervirens

Calceolaria

Common Name: Slipper flower, Florist's slipperwort

Plant Notes: Pronounced 'Kal-see-oh-LAIR-re-uh'. A pretty flowering plant with large, soft leaves and brightly coloured petals that fuse together to form a slipper-shaped pouch. Can go outside in the summer as part of a bedding scheme.

Type: Flowering annual.
Colour: Bright yellow, orange, with red spots.
Ideal Spot: Warm sunny windowsill.
Height: Small. 30cm/12".
Skill Level: Easy.
Longevity: Annual.

Essential Care:
- **Temperature:** Cool/warm. 10–15°C/50–60°F.
- **Watering:** Keep compost moist, but not waterlogged.
- **Humidity:** Medium. Mist weekly, avoid wetting flowers.
- **Light:** Bright but shield from direct sun.
- **Feeding:** Every two weeks during flowering.

General Care:
- Flowering period, early to late spring.
- Standing the plant in a pebble tray will improve humidity.
- Once it has finished flowering – recycle!
- Suitable for pots and baskets but not frost hardy.

Troubleshooting:
- Plant collapse; soggy compost.

Pests & Diseases:
- Prone to aphid attack.

Trivia:
C. *x herbeohybrida*, more commonly known as Florist's Slipperwort, is the only Calceolaria bred specifically for the indoor pot plant market.

Family: Calceolariaceae.
Genus: Calceolaria.
Origin: Central America.

C. *x herbeohybrida*

Canna

Common Name: **Indian shot plant**

Plant Notes: Pronounced 'CAN-na'. Dramatic and colourful, the dazzling flowers of this exotic plant are perfectly set off by its equally striking green/burgundy foliage. Often used as the crowning glory of an outdoor bedding scheme.

Type: Flowering perennial.
Colour: Fiery red, orange, yellow, pink.
Ideal Spot: Cool conservatory, sunny patio.
Height: Tall. Up to 1.8m/6'.
Skill Level: Average.
Longevity: Perennial.

Essential Care:
- **Temperature:** Cool/warm. 7–15°C/45–60°F.
- **Watering:** Freely when in flower.
- **Humidity:** Medium. Mist every 3 to 4 days.
- **Light:** Bright, sunny position.
- **Feeding:** Feed monthly while in flower.

General Care:
- Flowers June to October. Can be placed outside.
- Deadhead to encourage repeat flowering.
- When flower spike has finished, prune down to next side shoot to encourage a second flower spike.

Troubleshooting:
- Failure to flower; either compost is too dry or of poor quality.

Pests & Diseases:
- Red spider mite, aphids.

After Flowering:
Move pot into a frost-free place, cut back leaves and reduce watering to almost nothing, allowing the rhizome to rest. The rhizome can also be dug up and stored in damp peat over winter.

Family: Cannaceae.
Genus: Canna.
Origin: Tropical Americas.

Canna

Capsicum

Common Name: **Christmas pepper**

Plant Notes: Pronounced 'CAP-se-come'. Decorative and compact, Capsicums are ideal for autumn and Christmas planted arrangements. Their fruits, which are initially green will change colour as they mature.

Type: Decorative houseplant.
Colour: Glossy red, yellow, orange and purple fruits.
Ideal Spot: Bright windowsill.
Height: Small. 30cm/12".
Skill Level: Easy.
Longevity: Fruits up to 3 months.

Essential Care:
- **Temperature:** Cool/warm. 10–18°C/50–65°F.
- **Watering:** Use immersion method, letting compost dry out slightly in between.
- **Humidity:** Low. Mist leaves weekly, avoid getting fruits wet.
- **Light:** Bright, sunny position.
- **Feeding:** Weekly.

General Care:
- Produces its fruits late autumn and winter.
- A well-lit spot will keep its colour bright.
- Once fruits have gone over, recycle.

Troubleshooting:
- Hot dry air or insufficient light will cause fruit to fall.
- Leaf drop; too warm.
- Plant collapse; overwatering.

Pests & Diseases:
- Aphids and red spider mite, botrytis.

In Design Work:
Fruits can be cut from the plant and wired into floral foam for seasonal arrangements. Add whole plants into mixed planted designs to add texture and a splash of bright colour.

Family: Solanaceae.
Genus: Capsicum.
Origin: Central & South America.

Capsicum annuum

Celosia

Common Name: **Chinese wool flower, Cockscomb**

Plant Notes: Pronounced 'See-LO-see-uh'. The vibrant, jewel coloured flowers of Celosia are hard to resist. Suitable for both indoors and outside where they will be a vibrant addition to summer bedding schemes.

Type: Flowering houseplant.
Colour: Pink, red, yellow, purple, orange.
Ideal Spot: Well-lit windowsill.
Height: Small. 30cm/12".
Skill Level: Easy.
Longevity: Annual.

Essential Care:
- **Temperature:** Cool/warm. 10–18°C/50–65°F.
- **Watering:** Always keep compost moist.
- **Humidity:** Low. Mist leaves occasionally, avoid wetting flowers.
- **Light:** Bright but shade from direct sunlight.
- **Feeding:** Every two weeks while in flower.

C. argentea

General Care:
- Main flowering period April to September.
- Can be added into containers outside but is not frost hardy.
- Once they have finished flowering – recycle!

Troubleshooting:
- Plant collapse can be caused by overwatering.

Pests & Diseases:
- Red spider mite and aphids.

Trivia:
In Nigeria Celosia is a popular leafy green vegetable, where it is known as 'soko yokoto', meaning "make husbands fat and happy".

Family: Amaranthaceae.
Genus: Celosia.
Origin: Tropical regions.

Celosia cristata

Ceropegia

Common Name: **String of hearts, Rosary vine**

Plant Notes:	Pronounced 'Se-ro-PEE-gee-uh'. An interesting and attractive trailing plant with pretty, mottled heart-shaped leaves. Suitable for hanging baskets or can trained around a frame.
Type:	Succulent.
Colour:	Grey-green, purple, silver.
Ideal Spot:	Warm bright room.
Trails:	up to 90cm/36".
Skill Level:	Easy.
Longevity:	5 + years.

Essential Care:

- **Temperature:** Warm/hot. 18–24°C/65–75°F.
- **Watering:** Keep compost moist to slightly dry, never soggy.
- **Humidity:** Low. Misting not necessary, but they appreciate fresh air.
- **Light:** Bright but protect from hot summer sun.
- **Feeding:** Monthly in spring and summer only.

General Care:

- Ceropegia lie dormant in winter so water sparingly.
- They can withstand a certain amount of neglect.
- To propagate, take cuttings from the stem tips and insert into moist compost.

Troubleshooting:

- Wilting leaves; compost is too wet.

Pests & Diseases:

- Relatively free of pests and diseases.

> **In Design Work:**
> Ceropegia are extremely versatile. They can be used for winding or veiling, and individual leaves can be detached and cold glued for floral jewellery.

Family: Apocynaceae.
Genus: Ceropegia.
Origin: South Africa.

Ceropegia linearis subsp. *woodii*

Chamaedorea

Common Name: **Parlour palm, Good luck palm**

Plant Notes: Pronounced 'Sham-a-DOOR-re-uh'. An attractive plant, the slim stems of this bushy palm bear large elegant pinnate leaves.

Type: Palm.
Colour: Dark glossy green.
Ideal Spot: Shady living room.
Height: Medium: 60cm/24".
Skill Level: Easy.
Longevity: 10 + years.

Essential Care:
- **Temperature:** Warm. 12–18°C/53–65°F.
- **Watering:** Keep moist but allow to dry out slightly between watering.
- **Humidity:** Medium. Mist if in a heated room and avoid draughts.
- **Light:** Prefers partial shade, avoid direct sunlight.
- **Feeding:** Monthly in spring and summer.

General Care:
- Never cut back stems as the growing point is at the tip.
- Clean dusty leaves with a damp cloth.
- Benefits from winter rest, reduce watering and move to a cooler spot.

Troubleshooting:
- Brown tips mean the air is too dry.
- Yellowing leaves; underwatering.

Pests & Diseases:
- Susceptible to red spider mite, scale insects and thrips.

Trivia:
Very similar is the Howea or Kentia palm which is taller and has slightly wider leaflets, although its care is the same. It lacks the delicateness and compactness of the Chamaedorea.

Family: Arecaceae.
Genus: Chamaedorea.
Origin: Mexico & Guatemala.

Chamaedorea elegans
Syn. *Neanthe bella*

Chamaerops

Common Name: Dwarf/European fan palm

Plant Notes: Pronounced 'SHAM-a-rops'. This shrubby palm with stiff, pinnate leaves is an excellent specimen plant which can go outside in the summer.
Type: Palm.
Colour: Dark green.
Ideal Spot: Large sitting room or conservatory.
Height: Medium/tall. 1.5–3m/4–9'.
Skill Level: Easy.
Longevity: 10 + years.

Essential Care:
- **Temperature:** Cool/warm. 7–21°C/45–70°F.
- **Watering:** Generously in summer, avoid over soaking.
- **Humidity:** Low. Mist if in a heated room and keep out of draughts.
- **Light:** Prefers partial shade, avoid direct sunlight.
- **Feeding:** Once a month spring and summer.

General Care:
- Can withstand low temperatures but protect from frost.
- Misting regularly will help to keep pests at bay.
- Avoid leafshine, clean dusty leaves with a damp cloth.

Troubleshooting:
- Brown tips on leaves; too dry or scorched by sun.

Pests & Diseases:
- Red spider mite if air indoors is too dry.
- Can develop false smut on leaves.

Trivia:
Slow growing and architectural in structure, Chamaerops is the world's most northerly, naturally occurring palm and is one of only two species native to Europe.

Family: Arecaceae.
Genus: Chamaerops.
Origin: Southern Europe.

Chamaerops humulis

Chlorophytum

Common Name: Spider plant, Airplane plant

Plant Notes: Pronounced 'Klo-ro-FY-tum'. A hugely popular houseplant, with grassy, variegated foliage and a cascading habit. It produces small, white star-shaped flowers on long stems.

Type: Foliage houseplant.
Colour: Mid/bright green, cream and white stripes.
Ideal Spot: Hanging basket or bright windowsill.
Trails: 60–90cm/2–3'.
Skill Level: Easy.
Longevity: 5 + years.

CO_2

Essential Care:
- **Temperature:** 10–18°C/50–65°F.
- **Watering:** Liberally in spring and summer, less so in winter.
- **Humidity:** Medium. Mist every 2 to 3 days.
- **Light:** Enjoys a well-lit spot, out of direct sunlight.
- **Feeding:** Every two weeks spring to autumn.

General Care:
- Propagate offsets by potting them up while still attached to the main plant, cut them free when they start to show new shoots.
- Old untidy leaves can be trimmed off.

Troubleshooting:
- Brown slimy marks in centre of plant; too wet.
- Brittle leaves will be damaged by wiping.

Pests & Diseases:
- Dry air can attract red spider mite.

Trivia:
The humble spider plant is in NASA's top ten of air purifying plants. They have been used as a biological life support system aboard orbiting space stations.

Family: Asparagaceae.
Genus: Chlorophytum.
Origin: South Africa.

Chlorophytum comosum

Chrysanthemum

Common Name: **Mum, Pot mum**

Plant Notes: Pronounced 'Cree-SAN-thee-mum'. Traditional but cheerful and free flowering in a wide range of colours. It may be short lived as an indoor plant, but it has an old-fashioned charm which is hard to resist.

CO_2

Type:	Flowering houseplant.	**Size:**	Small/medium. 20–60cm/8–24".
Colour:	All except for blue and purple.	**Skill Level:**	Easy.
Ideal Spot:	Bright windowsill or outside patio.	**Longevity:**	Flowers for 6–8 weeks.

Essential Care:
- **Temperature:** Cool. 10–15°C/50–60°F.
- **Watering:** Keep compost moist, but not wet.
- **Humidity:** Low. Spray lightly occasionally.
- **Light:** Bright, but out of direct sunlight.
- **Feeding:** Weekly while in flower.

General Care:
- Main flowering period March to October.
- When buying, check that there are plenty of buds.
- Deadhead to prolong flowering.
- Can go outside in the summer.
- Once flowering has finished, recycle or plant in the garden.

Troubleshooting:
- Wilting leaves; underwatering.
- Failure to flower; not enough light.
- Short flowering period; too warm.

Pests & Diseases:
- Aphids, red spider mite, botrytis.

> **Trivia:**
> Chrysanthemums rate very highly with NASA for removing formaldehyde, benzene and ammonia from the atmosphere. There are Pot mums in space…

Family: Asteraceae.
Genus: Chrysanthemum.
Origin: Asia & N/E Europe.

Chrysanthemum spp.

Cissus

Common Name: **Grape ivy**

Plant Notes: Pronounced 'SIS-us'. A vigorous, evergreen climber, which can be used to cover walls and trelliswork. *C. antarctica* have large, serrated leaves, while *C. rhombifolia* are smaller and more decorative.

Type: Foliage trailer/climber.
Colour: Rich, glossy green.
Ideal Spot: Large conservatory or porch.
Height: Tall. 2m/6'.
Skill Level: Easy.
Longevity: 10 + years.

Essential Care:
- **Temperature:** Warm/hot. 15–24°C/60–75°F.
- **Watering:** Freely in summer, less frequently in winter.
- **Humidity:** Low. Mist every two weeks.
- **Light:** Indirect light, will tolerate some shade.
- **Feeding:** Monthly, spring to autumn.

General Care:
- Minimum winter temperature 10°C/50°F.
- Easy to train up frameworks and trellis.
- Also suitable for hanging baskets.
- Avoid using leafshine, clean leaves with a damp cloth.

Troubleshooting:
- Shedding leaves; air is too dry.
- Brown/brittle leaves; over exposure to hot sun.

Pests & Diseases:
- Aphids, whitefly and red spider mite.

> **Winter Care:**
> Stop feeding and reduce watering. Cutting it back in early spring and keeping it slightly pot bound will help to keep its shape and curb its vigorousness.

Family: Vitaceae.
Genus: Cissus.
Origin: Tropical Americas.

Cissus rhombifolia

Citrus

Common Name: Orange, Lemon, Lime, Kumquat

Plant Notes: Pronounced 'SIT-truss'. Ornamental plants with glossy oval leaves and creamy, scented flowers in summer which, given the right conditions, will develop into fruits.

Type: Fruiting houseplant.
Colour: Glossy green; orange, lemon, lime fruits.
Ideal Spot: Sunny conservatory, patio or porch.
Height: Medium/tall. 60–90cm/24–36".
Skill Level: Average.
Longevity: 5 + years.

Essential Care:
- **Temperature:** Cool/warm. 10–15°C/50–60°F.
- **Watering:** Keep compost moist using soft water or rainwater.
- **Humidity:** Medium. Mist leaves weekly.
- **Light:** Bright, sunny position.
- **Feeding:** Weekly spring and summer, less in winter.

General Care:
- Place outside in summer in a sunny position.
- Pinch out tips of branches to maintain bushy plants.
- Cut fruits rather than pull them off the plant.

Troubleshooting:
- No signs of growth; too cold.
- Leaf loss or leaves with brown tips; too draughty.
- Yellowing leaves are a sign of magnesium deficiency.

Pests & Diseases:
- Scale insects, red spider mite, aphids.

Pollination:
For Citrus to fruit, they will need pollinating. This will occur naturally if the plant is outside. If inside, use a small paint brush to transfer pollen onto the stigma.

Family: Rutaceae.
Genus: Citrus.
Origin: Asia.

Citrus reticulata
Syn. x *Citrofortunella*

Clivia

Common Name: Kaffir lily, Natal lily

Plant Notes: Pronounced 'KLIV-e-uh'. Dramatic with dark green, glossy leaves which rise from the base of the plant. It produces clusters of up to 20 bell shaped, vibrantly coloured flowers in spring and summer.

Type: Flowering houseplant.
Colour: Dark green, fiery orange, red, yellow.
Ideal Spot: Bright sitting room or conservatory.
Height: Medium. 60cm/24".
Skill Level: Expert.
Longevity: 5 + years.

Essential Care:
- **Temperature:** Warm/hot. 15–21°C/60–70°F in summer.
- **Watering:** Weekly when growing and in flower.
- **Humidity:** Medium. Sponge leaves with tepid water.
- **Light:** Bright but out of direct sunlight.
- **Feeding:** Weekly in growing and flowering period.

General Care:
- Once in bud, don't move the plant or they will shed.
- Keep out of draughts.
- Can be placed outside in summer.

Troubleshooting:
- Failure to flower; insufficient resting period.
- Flowers failing to form; too warm.

Pests & Diseases:
- Mealy bugs; root rot if overwatered.

After Flowering:
It is vital that Clivia have a resting period. Move the plant to a cool room with a temperature range of 7–10°C/45–50°F. Feed and water sparingly. Move to a warmer position once buds start to form.

Family: Amaryllidaceae.
Genus: Clivia.
Origin: South Africa.

Clivia miniata

Cocos

Common Name: **Coconut palm, Malayan coconut palm**

Plant Notes: Pronounced 'Co-COS'. Elegant with long, graceful leaves, these palms are more suited to white sandy beaches than being a domestic houseplant, but they will tolerate indoor conditions.

Type: Palm.
Colour: Dark glossy green.
Ideal Spot: Large warm conservatory or porch.
Height: Tall. 1.8m/5'.
Skill Level: Expert.
Longevity: 1–2 years.

Essential Care:
- **Temperature:** Hot. 18–24°C /65–75°F.
- **Watering:** Keep compost moist, needs good drainage.
- **Humidity:** Medium. Mist if in a heated room.
- **Light:** Sunny but shade from direct sunlight.
- **Feeding:** In summer while plant is growing.

General Care:
- Prefers tepid water and well drained sandy compost.
- Keep away from draughts.
- Clean dusty leaves with a damp cloth, avoid leafshine.

Troubleshooting:
- Yellowing leaves can be caused by underwatering.
- Brown leaves; air is too dry.

Pests & Diseases:
- Red spider mite, scale insects and mealy bugs.

Trivia:
When immature, coconuts; also known as 'tender-nuts' or 'jelly-nuts' can be harvested for drinking. Dried coconut flesh is known as 'copra'.

Family: Arecaceae.
Genus: Cocos.
Origin: Tropics.

Cocos nucifera

Codiaeum

Common Name: **Croton, Joseph's coat**

Plant Notes: Pronounced 'Koe-dee-EE-um'. Vividly coloured, wavy edged leaves are marked with prominent veins in contrasting shades. Bushy, with thick, leathery foliage and an upright habit.

Type: Foliage houseplant.
Colour: Gold, yellow, pink, red, purple, orange.
Ideal Spot: Warm conservatory; east/west window.
Height: Medium. 60cm/24".
Skill Level: Expert.
Longevity: 5 + years.

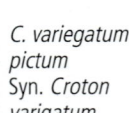

Essential Care:
- **Temperature:** Warm/hot. 18–27°C/65–80°F.
- **Watering:** Keep moist using tepid water, spring to autumn.
- **Humidity:** High. Spray air around plant daily, use pebble tray.
- **Light:** Good, bright light, protect from direct sun.
- **Feeding:** Every two weeks in summer.

General Care:
- Keep out of draughts and cold spots.
- Wipe leaves with a damp cloth, avoid using leafshine.
- Dislikes sudden changes in its environment.

Troubleshooting:
- Tips or edges of leaves brown, air is too cool or dry.
- Leaf drop; lack of humidity and warmth.
- Loss of leaf colour; needs more light.

Pests & Diseases:
- Red spider mite and scale insects.

Winter Care:
Rest during winter with a minimum temperature of 15°C/60°F. Reduce watering and stop feeding. It will naturally lose many of its leaves during this time. For this reason, it is often grown as an annual.

C. variegatum pictum
Syn. *Croton varigatum*

Family: Euphorbiaceae.
Genus: Codiaeum.
Origin: S/E Asia & Northern Australia.

Coffea

Common Name: **Coffee tree**

Plant Notes: Pronounced 'Koff-e-uh.' Attractive, with dark green shiny leaves that have slightly wavy edges. More established plants bear white scented flowers in spring followed by small berries.

Type: Foliage houseplant.
Colour: Dark, glossy green.
Ideal Spot: Any room but keep out of draughts.
Height: Medium. 60cm/24".
Skill Level: Easy.
Longevity: 5 + years.

Essential Care:
- **Temperature:** Warm/hot. 18–24°C/65–75°F.
- **Watering:** Keep compost moist, but not waterlogged.
- **Humidity:** Low. Mist weekly.
- **Light:** Bright but avoid direct sunlight.
- **Feeding:** Once a month.

General Care:
- Prune lightly in spring to keep it in shape.
- Dislikes being in a draught.
- Clean leaves with a damp cloth.
- Minimum winter temperature of 10°C/50°F.

Troubleshooting:
- Wilting leaves; check plant is not in a draught.

Pests & Diseases:
- Not especially prone to pests or diseases.

Trivia:
It is possible to grow Coffea from an unroasted coffee bean, although It might be a few years before you could harvest any coffee!

Family: Rubiaceae.
Genus: Coffea.
Origin: Yemen.

Coffea arabica

Cordyline

Common Name: **False palm, Good luck plant, Ti plant**

Plant Notes: Pronounced 'KOR-de-line'. Often forming the central display in a planted patio container, Cordyline also make attractive plants for inside where they will bring a little of the outdoors, indoors.

Type: Foliage houseplant.
Colour: Dark/mid green, bronze, red, pink.
Ideal Spot: Sunny room or patio.
Height: Tall. 90cm/36".
Skill Level: Easy.
Longevity: 2–5 years.

Essential Care:
- **Temperature:** Warm. 13–18°C/55–65°F.
- **Watering:** Keep compost moist, reduce watering in winter.
- **Humidity:** High. Mist every 3 to 4 days, use pebble tray.
- **Light:** Happiest in light shade.
- **Feeding:** Weekly in summer.

General Care:
- Protect from direct sunlight.
- Sensitive to cold and draughts.
- Can go outside in summer.
- Not frost hardy, so overwinter indoors.

Troubleshooting:
- Brown tips on leaves; air too dry.
- Plant collapse; overwatering.

Pests & Diseases:
- Not especially prone to pests and diseases.

Trivia:
Cordyline are very similar to Dracaena, to tell the difference look at the roots, the former has white roots, the latter a deep yellow.

Family: Asparagaceae.
Genus: Cordyline.
Origin: Pacific Ocean region.

Cordyline fruticosa

Cotyledon

Common Name: **Silver crown, Silver ruffles**

Plant Notes: Pronounced 'kot-e-LEE-don''. A pretty succulent with scalloped shaped leaves some of which have a light silvery bloom, they bear pink or yellow flowers in summer.

Type: Succulent.
Colour: Blue/grey, grey/white.
Ideal Spot: Sunny windowsill.

Height: Small: 30cm/12".
Skill Level: Easy.
Longevity: 2–5 years.

Essential Care:
- **Temperature:** Cool to hot. 6–30°C/42–86°F.
- **Watering:** Thoroughly when compost dries out; reduce watering in winter.
- **Humidity:** Low. Misting is not necessary but fresh air is important.
- **Light:** Bright, will tolerate some direct sunshine.
- **Feeding:** Every two weeks in spring and summer.

General Care:
- Don't water from above, as this will wash off the 'icing sugar' effect from the leaves.
- For the same reason, avoid using leafshine and misting leaves.

Troubleshooting:
- A leggy plant needs more light.
- Plant rot; overwatering.

Pests & Diseases:
- Susceptible to mealy bugs.

Cotyledon undulata

Trivia:
Found on rocky ground and on cliff faces in their natural habitat, the fleshy leaves of the plant have been used in the past as treatment for corns.

Family: Crassulaceae.
Genus: Cotyledon.
Origin: Southern Africa.

Crassula

Common Name: Money/Silver dollar plant, Jade plant

Plant Notes: Pronounced 'KRASS-you-lar'. A very large and varied plant group. The one most commonly available as a houseplant is *C. ovata* which has paddle shaped leaves and tree like growth.

Type: Succulent.
Colour: Green with red margins.
Ideal Spot: Warm, bright room.
Height: Small to tall. 30–90cm/12–36".
Skill Level: Easy.
Longevity: 10 + years.

Essential Care:
- **Temperature:** Warm/hot. 15–27°C/60–80°F.
- **Watering:** Water sparingly, allowing plant to dry out in between.
- **Humidity:** Low. Misting is not necessary, but they appreciate fresh air.
- **Light:** Bright, will tolerate some direct sunlight.
- **Feeding:** Every two weeks during spring and summer.

General Care:
- Can be placed outside on warm summer days.
- Appreciates a contrast between day and night temperatures.
- Remove dead leaves regularly.
- Clean leaves with water and a damp cloth.

Troubleshooting:
- Using tepid water can cause leaf fall.
- Needs good ventilation to prevent leaf spot disease.

Pests & Diseases:
- Prone to mealy bugs.

Winter Care:
Provide winter rest in a cool room, minimum of 7°C/45°F. Stop feeding and reduce watering to almost nothing, the leaves will have stored water from the previous season.

Family: Crassulaceae.
Genus: Crassula.
Origin: Western Cape & South Africa.

Crassula ovata
Syn. *C. argentea*

Cryptanthus

Common Name: **Earth star**

Plant Notes: Pronounced 'Krypt-AN-thus.' A distinctive rosette shaped plant with strap-like leaves marked by either bold ripples or stripes of colour. Low growing, they produce fragrant white flowers in summer.

Type: Bromeliad.
Colour: Shades of green, red, cream and bronze.
Ideal Spot: Terrarium, kitchen, bathroom.
Height: Small. 10–25cm/4–10".
Skill Level: Easy.
Longevity: 5 + years.

Essential Care:
- **Temperature:** Warm/hot. 15–27°C/60–80°F.
- **Watering:** Don't overwater; keep slightly dry, rainwater is preferable.
- **Humidity:** Medium. Mist lightly in warm weather.
- **Light:** Indirect light, will tolerate semi-shade.
- **Feeding:** Add liquid plant food every 2 to 3 months.

General Care:
- A shallow root system means that overwatering can be fatal.
- The leaves are slightly serrated, handle with care.
- Avoid direct sunlight as this will fade leaf colours.

Troubleshooting:
- Plant collapse; too wet.
- Brown tips are caused by dry air.

Pests & Diseases:
- Susceptible to scale insects and mealy bugs.

Propagation:
The mother plant will produce 'pups'. These can be carefully removed once they have developed leaves and re-potted into a mix of orchid and multipurpose compost. See page 133.

Family: Bromeliaceae.
Genus: Cryptanthus.
Origin: Brazil.

C. bivittatus 'Red Star'

Curio

Common Name: **String of pearls, Senecio**

Plant Notes: Pronounced 'Que-ri-oh.' A fascinating plant with unusual pearl shaped leaves which will trail elegantly down the side of a tall container or hanging basket. Easy to care for, this is a great plant for a novice.

Type: Succulent.
Colour: Sage green.
Ideal Spot: Sunny position with room to trail.

Trails: Up to 90cm/36".
Skill Level: Easy.
Longevity: 5 + years.

Essential Care:

- **Temperature:** Warm/hot. 10–30°C/50–86°F.
- **Watering:** Keep compost moist spring to autumn, reduce watering in winter.
- **Humidity:** Low. Fresh air is more important.
- **Light:** Bright and sunny but shade from direct sun in high summer.
- **Feeding:** Annually in late spring.

General Care:

- Allow the plant to dry out slightly between watering.
- The 'strings' are quite brittle, handle with care.
- Trim back annually to keep the plant in check and in shape.

Troubleshooting:

- Beads turning brown; sun scorch.
- Plant rot; overwatering.

Pests & Diseases:

- Relatively free from pests and diseases.

Trivia:
In its native habitat Curio grows on rocky outcrops in full sun. The tiny circular leaves hold water which is crucial for its survival.

Family: Asteraceae.
Genus: Curio.
Origin: South Namibia.

Curio rowleyanus
Syn. *Senecio rowleyanus*

Cycas

Common Name: **Sago palm**

Plant Notes: Pronounced 'SI-kas'. Rosettes of stiff, deeply divided leaves sprout in a circular arrangement out of a rough, solid trunk. Architecturally interesting, often found as part of commercial landscaping schemes.

Type: Foliage houseplant.
Colour: Dark to mid green.
Ideal Spot: Large living room or conservatory.
Height: Medium. 60cm/24".
Skill Level: Easy.
Longevity: 10 + years.

Essential Care:
- **Temperature:** Cool to hot. 13–24°C/55–75°F.
- **Watering:** Keep compost moist during growing period.
- **Humidity:** High. Mist daily if air is especially dry.
- **Light:** Prefers partial shade.
- **Feeding:** Monthly spring to autumn.

General Care:
- Don't let the plant sit in water.
- Sponge leaves carefully to remove dust.
- Reduce watering in winter.

Troubleshooting:
- Overwatering will cause root rot.
- Brown tips or yellowing leaves mean air is too dry.
- Brown spots can be caused by using hard water.

Pests & Diseases:
- Susceptible to red spider mite when indoors.

> **Trivia:**
> Extremely slow growing, sometimes putting out only one leaf a year. Despite its common name, it is not related to the palm family.

Family: Cycadaceae.
Genus: Cycas.
Origin: Southern Japan & China.

Cycas revoluta

Cyclamen

Common Name: **Florist's Cyclamen**

Plant Notes: Pronounced 'Sic-LA-men'. A popular and pretty flowering plant with distinctive silver marbling on its leaves and dramatic, swept back petals. Some have a soft, sweet scent.

Type: Flowering houseplant.
Colour: Pure white, pale pink to deep red.
Ideal Spot: Cool room or windowsill.
Height: Small. 15–30cm/6–12".
Skill Level: Average.
Longevity: 2 + years.

Essential Care:
- **Temperature:** Cool/warm. 10–18°C/50–65°F.
- **Watering:** Use immersion method with soft water.
- **Humidity:** Low. Mist air around plant, not directly onto leaves and flowers.
- **Light:** Indirect, keep out of bright sunshine.
- **Feeding:** Weekly during flowering period.

General Care:
- Never let the plant stand in water and always water from below.
- Keep out of draughts and sudden changes in temperature.
- Remove old leaves and flowers as they die back.

Troubleshooting:
- Plant collapse; overwatering.
- Yellowing leaves; too hot, or dry.

Pests & Diseases:
- Botrytis, whitefly.
- Cyclamen mite; if affected the plant should be destroyed.

After Flowering:
Naturally winter flowering, Cyclamen will die down in the spring. Once dormant stop watering and place in a cool spot to allow the plant's corm to dry out. Repot in fresh compost at midsummer and resume feed and watering.

Family: Primulaceae.
Genus: Cyclamen.
Origin: Mediterranean & North Africa.

Cyclamen persicum

Cymbidium

Common Name: **Cymbidium, Boat orchid**

Plant Notes:	Pronounced 'Sim-BID-ee-um.' Popular since Victorian times, this large, showy orchid will flower for months in the right conditions.
Type:	Orchid.
Colour:	All except for red, blue and purple.
Ideal Spot:	A sunny room, not heated at night.
Height:	Tall. 90cm/36".
Skill Level:	Average.
Longevity:	5 + years.

Essential Care:

- **Temperature:** Warm/hot. 10–25°C/50–77°F.
- **Watering:** Water with distilled or rainwater allowing compost to dry out slightly in between.
- **Humidity:** Medium. Mist leaves every 3 to 4 days, stand in pebble tray.
- **Light:** Bright, well-lit spot, out of direct sunlight.
- **Feeding:** Every two weeks spring and summer with specialised orchid feed.

General Care:

- Seasonal; flowering period late autumn to spring.
- Needs a cool night temperature, maximum of 15°C/60°F.
- Avoid leaving the plant overnight in a centrally heated room.
- Appreciates fresh air, stand plant outside in summer.

Troubleshooting:

- No flowers? Either not enough light or too warm and dry, move to an unheated room or place outside.
- Bud drop; too warm at night and inadequate light.

Pests & Diseases:

- Can develop mildew if air is too damp.

After Flowering:
Cut the old flower spikes off at the base and move to a greenhouse or porch where the plant will have the benefits of warm days and cool nights. Keeping it slightly pot bound will also encourage it to re-flower.

Family: Orchidaceae.
Genus: Cymbidium.
Origin: South-East Asia.

Cymbidium spp.

Cyperus

Common Name: **Umbrella plant/grass**

Plant Notes: Pronounced 'SI-per-us'. A natural marshland plant with stiff, grassy leaves ranging from very fine to broad, which radiate from a central point. It has insignificant green/brown flowers.

Type: Foliage houseplant.
Colour: Dark to mid green.
Ideal Spot: Large, warm, humid room.
Height: Tall. 90cm/36".
Skill Level: Easy.
Longevity: 5 + years.

Essential Care:
- **Temperature:** Warm. 10–21°C/50–70°F.
- **Watering:** Always keep compost wet, will need less water in winter.
- **Humidity:** High. Mist leaves and air around the plant daily.
- **Light:** Sunny or partial shade.
- **Feeding:** Every two weeks during summer months.

General Care:
- Stand plant in a container of shallow water which should be changed daily.
- Remove yellowing stems to encourage new growth.

Troubleshooting:
- Brown tips on leaves; plant is too dry.

Pests & Diseases:
- Relatively pest and disease free.

Trivia:
According to the Bible, Cyperus was the material used for the basket that carried Moses down the river Nile.

Family: Cyperaceae.
Genus: Cyperus.
Origin: Subtropical Africa.

Cyperus haspan

Dendrobium

Common Name: Singapore orchid

Plant Notes: Pronounced 'Den-DROW-be-um.' This delicate orchid is part of a huge genera, estimated at over 1000 different species. With a small root system, it prefers to be kept slightly pot bound.

Type: Orchid.
Colour: All except for blue and black.
Ideal Spot: Bright, shaded windowsill.
Height: Medium. 45–60cm/18–24".
Skill Level: Average.
Longevity: 5 + years.

Essential Care:
- **Temperature:** Warm/hot. 18–24°C/65–75°F.
- **Watering:** Weekly, letting growing medium dry out slightly in between.
- **Humidity:** High. Spray every 2 to 3 days, also needs good air circulation.
- **Light:** A bright or semi-shaded spot out of direct sunshine.
- **Feeding:** Weekly with diluted orchid fertilizer during growing period only.

General Care:
- Seasonal; flowering February to June.
- Lies dormant September to January, reduce watering and stop feeding to encourage buds to form.
- Winter minimum temperature of 10°C/50°F.
- Avoid placing the plant in draughts and cold spots.

Troubleshooting:
- No flowers? Insufficient light or winter care.
- Brown spots on leaves, sun scorch.

Pests & Diseases:
- Can develop mildew if conditions are too damp.

After flowering:
Cut back the flower sprays to the main stem and feed and water until the plant enters its dormant stage. If offsets are produced, this is the time to remove and repot them. See page 134.

Family: Orchidaceae.
Genus: Dendrobium.
Origin: Tropical Asia & Australia.

Dendrobium Berry 'Oda'

Dieffenbachia

Common Name: Dumb cane, Leopold lily

Plant Notes: Pronounced 'Diff-en-BACK-ee-uh.' Popular as a specimen plant with unmistakable large, boldly marked leaves, the Dieffenbachia never seems to go out of fashion despite its (deserved) difficult to keep reputation.

Type: Foliage houseplant.
Colour: Mid/bright green, cream variegation.
Ideal Spot: Warm porch or sitting room.
Height: Medium/tall. 60–90cm/24–36".
Skill Level: Expert.
Longevity: 3–4 years.

Essential Care:
- **Temperature:** Warm/hot. 15–24°C/60–75°F.
- **Watering:** Keep compost moist from spring to autumn.
- **Humidity:** High. Mist weekly and stand in pebble tray.
- **Light:** Partial shade in summer, bright light in winter.
- **Feeding:** Monthly from spring to autumn.

General Care:
- Will not tolerate low temperatures or draughts.
- Don't let compost become waterlogged, reduce watering in winter.
- Toxic, keep away from children and pets. Wash hands after touching plant.
- Old leaves will drop naturally with age.

Troubleshooting:
- Yellow leaves, stem slimy or rotting; too wet.
- Drooping leaves; the plant is too cold or in a draught.

Pests & Diseases:
- Scale insects and red spider mite.

> **Trivia:**
> The Strawberry poison-dart frog (*Oophago pumilio*) is known to use Dieffenbachia leaves as a safe haven to deposit its tadpoles.

> **Family:** Araceae.
> **Genus:** Dieffenbachia.
> **Origin:** Tropical Central & South America.

D. picta

Dracaena

Common Name: Ribbon plant

Plant Notes: Pronounced 'DRA-scene-na.' Often grown as a specimen, with attractive striped leaves sprouting from a thick woody trunk. Bold and decorative they make striking centrepieces in planted designs.

CO_2 ✗

Type: Foliage houseplant.
Colour: Striped in green, cream, pink and red.
Ideal Spot: Warm shady room or patio.
Height: Medium/tall. 90cm/36".
Skill Level: Easy.
Longevity: 5 + years.

Essential Care:
- **Temperature:** Warm/hot 15–24°C/60–75°F.
- **Watering:** Keep compost moist, don't let plant dry out.
- **Humidity:** High. Mist daily, they dislike dry air.
- **Light:** Prefers light shade or indirect light.
- **Feeding:** Every two weeks during summer.

General Care:
- Reduce watering in winter.
- Winter minimum of 12°C/55°F.
- Can go outside in summer months.

Troubleshooting:
- Brown tips or yellowing leaves mean air is too dry.

Pests & Diseases:
- Dry conditions can leave to red spider mite and mealy bugs.

Trivia:
Often confused with Cordyline, the difference is most obvious in the root stock. Dracaena roots are deep yellow, cordyline are white.

Family: Dracaenaceae.
Genus: Dracaena.
Origin: Tropical Africa.

Dracaena fragrans

Dracaena marginata

Echeveria

Common Name: **Hen and chicks, Moulded wax**

Plant Notes: Pronounced 'EK-ee-VE-re-uh.' Compact, rosette shaped succulent with tightly packed leaves, some with a white bloom, that have a symmetrical appeal. Arching stems bear small delicate flowers in summer.

Type: Succulent.	**Height:** Mini to medium. 15–60cm/6–24".
Colour: Pale green, pink, purple, grey.	**Skill Level:** Easy.
Ideal Spot: Sunny windowsill or dish garden.	**Longevity:** 10 + years.

Essential Care:
- **Temperature:** Cool to hot. 10–27°C/50–80°F.
- **Watering:** Keep compost moist in summer with tepid water.
- **Humidity:** Low. Misting not required, but they do appreciate fresh air.
- **Light:** Bright light, protect from direct sunlight.
- **Feeding:** Every two weeks in spring and summer.

General Care:
- Water sparingly in winter when the plant is resting.
- If displaying indoors, turn pots occasionally for even growth.
- Happy to be outside in summer but is not frost hardy.

Troubleshooting:
- Using cold water may result in sudden loss of leaves.
- Wilting plants in winter; compost is too wet.

Pests & Diseases:
- Mealy bugs and aphids.

In Design Work:
Popular in floristry, first wash roots clean of compost and carefully attach plant to a wooden pick which can then be added into modern design work.

Family: Crassulaceae.
Genus: Echeveria.
Origin: Mexico & Central America.

Echeveria agavoides

Euphorbia

Common Name: **Poinsettia, Christmas star**

Plant Notes: Pronounced 'U-FOR-bee-uh.' The quintessential Christmas houseplant with its unmistakable bright red and green colouring. Bushy and multi-stemmed, the vividly coloured leaves surround insignificant yellow flowers.

Type: Flowering houseplant.
Colour: Bright red, pink, marbled, cream.
Ideal Spot: Warm, draught free room.
Height: Small/medium. 20–60cm/8–24".
Skill Level: Average.
Longevity: Christmas season only.

Essential Care:
- **Temperature:** Warm/hot. 15–21°C/60–70°.
- **Watering:** Keep compost moist, don't let it dry out.
- **Humidity:** High. Needs moist air, spray frequently.
- **Light:** Plenty of bright light will maintain colour.
- **Feeding:** Not necessary over the short festive season.

General Care:
- Available November and December.
- Extremely sensitive to cold and draughts.
- Never buy a plant which has been displayed outside.
- Make sure plant is well wrapped up at purchase point.
- Once Christmas is over – recycle!

Troubleshooting:
- Leaf fall; overwatering, or too cold or too dark.

Pests & Diseases:
- Botrytis and whitefly.

After Flowering:
Euphorbia flowers naturally when days are shortest. It is possible to make it flower again, but it's very time consuming and best left to professional growers.

Family: Euphorbiaceae.
Genus: Euphorbia.
Origin: Mexico.

Euphorbia pulcherrima

Exacum

Common Name: **German/Persian/Arabian violet**

Plant Notes: Pronounced 'X-a-come'. With its compact growth habit, tiny, glossy leaves and delicate scented flowers, Exacum is an ideal indoor plant for small spaces. Available in both double and single varieties.

Type: Flowering houseplant.
Colour: White, lilac or purple with a yellow centre.
Ideal Spot: Bright windowsill away from draughts.
Height: Mini. 15cm/8".
Skill Level: Average.
Longevity: Annual.

Essential Care:
- **Temperature:** Warm/hot. 18–24°C/65–75°F.
- **Watering:** Keep compost moist but allow to dry out slightly in between watering.
- **Humidity:** High. Mist every 2 to 3 days, but don't over soak foliage.
- **Light:** Bright light, but away from direct sunlight.
- **Feeding:** Every two weeks when in flower.

General Care:
- Seasonal, flowering March to August.
- Display in a shallow container and deadhead regularly.
- Keep out of draughts.
- Can be recycled/discarded at end of flowering period.

Troubleshooting:
- Wilting plant; either in a draught or too dry.
- Constant humidity and bright light will encourage flowering.

Pests & Diseases:
- Not especially prone to pests or diseases.

Trivia:
Many ancient texts believe that Socotra (see below) was the original location for the Garden of Eden. Known as the 'Jewel of Arabia' it is Unesco protected.

Family: Gentianaceae.
Genus: Exacum.
Origin: Socotra Island, East Africa.

Exacum affine

x Fatshedera

Common Name: **Ivy tree**

Plant Notes: Pronounced 'Fats-HEAD-er-rah'. A cross between an ivy and a Fatsia, this is a reliable evergreen, if a little uninspiring. Its plus points are that it is undemanding and easy to care for.

Type: Foliage houseplant.
Colour: Dark/mid green.
Ideal Spot: Large cool porch or conservatory.
Height: Medium/tall. 45cm–2m/18"–6'.
Skill Level: Easy.
Longevity: 10 + years.

Essential Care:
- **Temperature:** Cool/warm. 10–15°C/50–60°F.
- **Watering:** Keep compost moist in summer, less so in winter.
- **Humidity:** Low. Mist every two weeks.
- **Light:** Bright light or semi-shade, protect from direct sun.
- **Feeding:** Every two weeks spring and summer.

General Care:
- Needs bright light in winter months, away from direct heat sources.
- Can go outside in summer in a shady spot.
- Will spread easily, pinch out leaf tips to retain shape.
- Wipe leaves occasionally to keep their glossy shine.

Troubleshooting:
- Soft, wilting leaves; too warm, choose an unheated room in winter.

Pests & Diseases:
- Red spider mite and botrytis.

Trivia:
The 'x' in the plants name indicates that it has deliberately been created from two different genera, in this case the 'parents' are *Fatsia japonica* and *Hedera helix*.

Family: Araliaceae.
Genus: x Fatshedera.
Origin: Nantes, France 1912.

x Fatshedera lizei

Fatsia

Common Name: Castor oil plant, Japanese Aralia

Plant Notes: Pronounced 'Phat-see-uh'. Reliable and robust, Fatsia is an excellent specimen plant with large, glossy leaves and an easy to look after reputation.

Type: Foliage houseplant.
Colour: Dark, glossy green. Some variegated.
Ideal Spot: Any spacious cool room or hallway.
Height: Medium/tall. Up to 2m/6'.
Skill Level: Easy.
Longevity: 15 + years.

Essential Care:
- **Temperature:** Cool/warm. 10–24°C/60–75°F.
- **Watering:** Keep compost moist spring and summer. Reduce watering in winter.
- **Humidity:** Medium. Mist every 2 to 3 days.
- **Light:** Bright or light shade. Protect from hot sun.
- **Feeding:** Every two weeks spring and summer.

General Care:
- Don't display near radiators or direct heat sources.
- Use a damp cloth to clean leaves.
- Benefits from being outside in summer.

Troubleshooting:
- Shrivelled leaves, too dry; increase humidity.
- Leaf drop; overwatering, especially in winter.

Pests & Diseases:
- Prone to scale insects, thrips and mealy bugs.

In Design Work:
The large palmate leaves can be used for arrangements in floral foam or for edging vase and hand tied designs. Condition for 24 hours before use.

Family: Araliaceae.
Genus: Fatsia.
Origin: Japan.

Fatsia japonica
Syn. *Aralia japonica*

Ficus benjamina

Common Name: Weeping fig

Plant Notes: Pronounced 'Fy-kus.' Graceful and treelike, this is an excellent specimen plant. Tall and slim, with slender oval leaves and a weeping habit it is most popular in its variegated form.

Type: Foliage houseplant.
Colour: Sage green with cream variegation.
Ideal Spot: Sunny conservatory or porch.

Height: Medium/tall. Up to 2m/6'.
Skill Level: Average.
Longevity: 5 + years.

Essential Care:
- **Temperature:** Warm/hot. 18–24°C/65–75°F.
- **Watering:** Tepid water, allow compost to dry out slightly between watering.
- **Humidity:** Low. Mist weekly in warm summer months.
- **Light:** Bright but avoid direct sunlight.
- **Feeding:** Every two weeks spring and summer.

General Care:
- Water more sparingly in winter.
- Needs a winter minimum temperature of 13°C/55°F.
- Dislikes draughts and being moved which can cause leaf drop.

Troubleshooting:
- Sudden loss of leaves; waterlogged compost, or too dark.
- Base leaves turning yellow and falling; this is a natural process.

Pests & Diseases:
- Relatively free from pests and diseases.

Trivia:
Ficus lyrata, or Fiddle-leaf fig enjoys the same care conditions as *F. benjamina*. It has large, violin shaped leaves and is capable of growing up to 1.2m/4'.

Family: Moraceae.
Genus: Ficus.
Origin: Israel.

Ficus benjamina

Ficus elastica

Common Name: **Rubber plant**

Plant Notes: Pronounced 'Fy-kus ee-LAST-te-ka'. One of the most recognisable and reliable of houseplants it has leathery, paddle shaped leaves and upright growing habit. Available in both green and variegated forms.

Type: Foliage houseplant.
Colour: Dark glossy green; pink & cream variegation.
Ideal Spot: Bright, large room.
Height: Tall. Up to 3m/10'.
Skill Level: Easy.
Longevity: 20 + years.

Essential Care:
- **Temperature:** Warm. 15–24°C/60–75°F.
- **Watering:** Use rainwater, allow to dry out slightly between watering.
- **Humidity:** Low. Mist occasionally and keep out of draughts.
- **Light:** Bright but shade from direct sunlight.
- **Feeding:** Weekly, spring and summer.

General Care:
- Water sparingly in winter.
- Winter minimum temperature 13°C/55°F.
- Wipe leaves occasionally with a damp cloth.
- The bottom leaves will naturally turn yellow and drop off with age.

Troubleshooting:
- Root rot or leaf drop; compost is too wet.
- Brown leaves can be caused by sun scorch.

Pests & Diseases:
- Mealy bugs, scale insects and red spider mite.

Trivia:
Capable of growing 30–40m in its natural habitat, in India the roots of the tree are sometimes trained across chasms to create a living bridge.

Family: Moraceae.
Genus: Ficus.
Origin: Asia.

Ficus elastica

Ficus pumila

Common Name: **Creeping fig**

Plant Notes: Pronounced 'Fi-Kus Pew-milla.' Wispy and delicate, this trailing member of the Ficus family is suitable for hanging baskets and terrariums. Available in both green and variegated forms.

Type: Foliage houseplant.
Colour: Sage green with cream margins.
Ideal Spot: Bathroom or shady porch.
Height: Medium. 60cm/24".
Skill Level: Average.
Longevity: 5 + years.

Essential Care:
- **Temperature:** Warm/hot. 18–24°C/65–75°F.
- **Watering:** Keep compost moist in spring and summer.
- **Humidity:** High. Mist daily in summer.
- **Light:** Indirect, or light shade.
- **Feeding:** Every two weeks spring and summer.

General Care:
- Rest over winter, reducing watering and feeding.
- Winter minimum temperature of 10°C/50°F.
- Sensitive to sudden changes in the environment.

Troubleshooting:
- Leaf drop; conditions are too dry or too cold.
- Shrivelled leaves; compost is too wet.

Pests & Diseases:
- Scale insects, red spider mite.

Trivia:
F. pumila can also be trained to climb moss poles and is useful ground cover in sheltered spots of the garden although it is not frost hardy.

Family: Moraceae.
Genus: Ficus.
Origin: East Asia.

Ficus pumila

Fittonia

Common Name: Snakeskin

Plant Notes:	Pronounced 'Fit-OWN-nee-uh.' Boldly marked leaves with colourful veins are typical of this delicate, low-growing creeping plant. Popular with the Victorians who were the first to introduced it as a houseplant.
Type:	Foliage houseplant.
Colour:	Olive green with white or red veining.
Ideal Spot:	Bathroom or terrarium.
Height:	Small. 30cm/12".
Skill Level:	Expert.
Longevity:	5 + years.

Essential Care:
- **Temperature:** Warm/hot. 18–24°C/65–75°F.
- **Watering:** Tepid water, keeping compost damp but not soggy.
- **Humidity:** High. Mist every 2 to 3 days and stand plant in pebble tray.
- **Light:** Partial shade, avoid direct sunlight.
- **Feeding:** Monthly, spring and summer.

General Care:
- Pinch out new growth to keep plant bushy.
- Avoid draughts, dry air and direct sunlight.
- Winter minimum temperature of 15°C/60°F.

Troubleshooting:
- Leaf drop; too cold or in a draught.
- Yellowing leaves; overwatering.
- Shrivelled leaves; air too dry or sun scorch.

Pests & Diseases:
- Can be prone to greenfly and botrytis.

Trivia:
The fact that this small, but demanding plant originates from the rain forests of Peru explains its love of warm, humid, shady conditions.

Family: Acantheceae.
Genus: Fittonia.
Origin: South America.

Fittonia argyroneura

Gardenia

Common Name: **Cape jasmine**

Plant Notes: Pronounced 'Guard-DIN-ee-uh.' A highly scented evergreen flowering plant with both single and double blooms. Very striking with tactile waxy flowers and glossy foliage.

Type: Flowering houseplant.
Colour: Dark green foliage, creamy flowers.
Ideal Spot: Warm conservatory, bathroom or porch.
Height: Medium. 60cm/24".
Skill Level: Expert.
Longevity: Up to 5 years.

Essential Care:
- **Temperature:** Warm/hot. 15–24°C/60–75°F.
- **Watering:** With rainwater, frequently in summer, less so in winter.
- **Humidity:** High. Mist weekly and use pebble tray. Avoid misting the flowers.
- **Light:** Bright, shade from direct sunlight.
- **Feeding:** Every two weeks, spring and summer.

General Care:
- Flowering season; summer to autumn.
- Minimum of 21°C/70°F (day) and 15°C/60°F (night) needed for flower buds to form.
- Winter minimum temperature of 12°C/55°F.
- Dislikes temperature fluctuations between day and night.
- For best results use ericaceous compost.

Troubleshooting:
- Bud drop; too dry, increase humidity.

Pests & Diseases:
- Mealy bugs and scale insects.

> **Trivia:**
> Gardenia are tricky to grow indoors. Using rainwater will help as it is naturally soft and contains less minerals, salts and chemical treatments.

Family: Rubiaceae.
Genus: Gardenia.
Origin: Tropical regions of Africa & Asia.

Gardenia jasminoides

Gerbera

Common Name: Gerbera, African daisy

Plant Notes: Pronounced 'JER-ber-uh.' Pretty, colourful daisy-like flowers on long, leafless stems, the gerbera plant is a colourful and welcome addition to any interior scheme.

CO_2

Type: Flowering houseplant.
Colour: All except green, purple and blue.
Ideal Spot: Sunny windowsill.
Height: Mini to medium. 15–60cm/6–24".
Skill Level: Easy.
Longevity: Perennial.

Essential Care:
- **Temperature:** Warm/hot. 10–21°C/50–70°F.
- **Watering:** Enough to keep compost moist without waterlogging.
- **Humidity:** Low. Mist every 2 to 3 weeks, wetting leaves only.
- **Light:** Bright, 3 to 4 hours a day, avoiding direct sunlight.
- **Feeding:** Weekly when in flower.

General Care:
- Seasonal; flowering from March to September.
- Appreciates good air circulation, can go outside in summer.
- Deadhead regularly to encourage new flowers.

Troubleshooting:
- Spots on leaves; lack of air circulation.
- Stem rot or flower collapse; too wet.

Pests & Diseases:
- Powdery mildew under wet conditions.

For arranging:
Using Gerbera plants in large floral installations is very effective, both visually and cost wise, particularly when arranged in blocks of strong colours.

Family: Asteraceae.
Genus: Gerbera.
Origin: South Africa.

Gerbera jamesonii

Goeppertia

Common Name: **Eternal flame, Calathea**

Plant Notes: Pronounced 'Go-ep-PER-tee-uh'. A member of the Maranta group, this rainforest plant is a quite a showstopper with its dramatic, dark coloured wavy leaves and bold spiky flowers.

Type: Flowering/foliage houseplant.
Colour: Orange and yellow flowers.
Ideal Spot: Humid spot; terrarium, bathroom.
Height: Medium. 60cm/24".
Skill Level: Expert.
Longevity: 2 + years.

Essential Care:
- **Temperature:** Warm/hot. 18–24°C/65–75°F.
- **Watering:** Keep compost moist but not wet, use tepid water.
- **Humidity:** High. Mist every 2 to 3 days and stand in pebble tray.
- **Light:** Indirect light; direct sun will damage leaves.
- **Feeding:** Every two weeks spring to autumn.

General Care:
- Don't allow compost to become waterlogged or let the plant stand in water.
- Very sensitive to temperature fluctuations and draughts.
- Clean leaves carefully with a damp cloth.
- Requires a winter minimum temperature of 17°C/60°F.

Troubleshooting:
- Leaf fall is a sign of a dry atmosphere.
- Yellowing/curling leaves indicates that compost is too dry.

Pests & Diseases:
- Prone to red spider mite.

> **Trivia:**
> In the same family are Ctenanthe, Stromanthe and Maranta (Prayer Plant). They are quite fussy with their requirements, but will reward the effort with their exotic, artistic foliage.

Family: Marantaceae.
Genus: Goeppertia.
Origin: Tropical America.

Goeppertia crocata.
Syn. *Calathea crocata*

Guzmania

Common Name: **Guzmania, Scarlet star**

Plant Notes: Pronounced 'Guze-MANE-ee-uh.' This easy to care for plant grows in a loose rosette shape from the centre of which emerges a brightly coloured spiky, star shaped bract.

Type: Bromeliad.
Colour: Orange, red, plum, yellow bracts.
Ideal Spot: Warm, light, sunny room.
Height: Medium. 30–60cm/12–24".
Skill Level: Average.
Longevity: 1–2 years.

Essential Care:
- **Temperature:** Warm/hot. 18–27°C/65–80°F.
- **Watering:** Add soft water or rainwater into central 'vase' of plant.
- **Humidity:** High. Mist daily during warm months.
- **Light:** Bright, natural light, shade from direct sun.
- **Feeding:** Feed monthly, misting with liquid food.

General Care:
- Will flower for four to six months in the right conditions.
- Keep compost moist allowing to it dry out in between.
- Flush out vase with fresh water every 1 to 2 months.
- Has a shallow root system for repotting, see page 133.

Troubleshooting:
- Plant collapse; overwatering.

Pests & Diseases:
- Relatively free from pests and diseases.

Trivia:
Named after Spanish adventurer and botanist, Anastasio Guzman who when searching for the lost gold of the Incas, stumbled across this Bromeliad instead.

Family: Bromeliaceae.
Genus: Guzmania.
Origin: W. Indies & Tropical Americas.

Guzmania lingulata

Haworthia

Common Name: Zebra cactus, Pearl plant

Plant Notes: Pronounced 'Haar-WUTH-e-uh.' Trim and neat in appearance with thick, firm leaves, many with a pretty pearl effect from tiny white nodules dotted over them. They are an ideal starter plant.

Type: Succulent.
Colour: Green with cream markings.
Ideal Spot: Any bright sunny room.
Height: Mini/small. 4–20cm/2–8".
Skill Level: Easy.
Longevity: 5 + years.

Essential Care:
- **Temperature:** Cool to hot. 5–27°C/41–80°F.
- **Watering:** Water when top of compost is dry, don't overwater.
- **Humidity:** Low. Not important.
- **Light:** Bright spot but out of direct sunlight.
- **Feeding:** Monthly, in spring only.

General Care:
- Recommend using cactus compost.
- Winter minimum temperature of 4°C/39°F.
- Reduce watering to a minimum over winter.
- Offsets from the main plant can be re-potted, see page 133.

Troubleshooting:
- Plant rot; overwatering.
- Plant shrivelling up; either too cold or too wet.

Pests & Diseases:
- Relatively free from pests and diseases.

In Design Work:
Use for adding texture into floral designs. Remove carefully from pot, shake off excess compost and tape onto a wooden pick. Can be re-potted after use.

Family: Asphodelaceae.
Genus: Haworthia.
Origin: Southern Africa.

Haworthia fasciata

Hedera

Common Name: **Ivy, Common/English ivy**

Plant Notes:	Pronounced 'Head-er-ra.' Reliable and dependable, ivy is often underrated as a houseplant. Practically standard fare in planted designs, while larger varieties make excellent specimen plants.	CO_2 ✗ ✂
Type:	Foliage houseplant.	**Trails:** 1.5–2m/6"–6'.
Colour:	Dark/mid green; white or cream variegation.	**Skill Level:** Easy.
Ideal Spot:	Unheated porches or conservatories.	**Longevity:** 10 + years.

Essential Care:
- **Temperature:** Cool. 10–15°C/50–60°F.
- **Watering:** Keep compost moist in summer, on the dry side in winter.
- **Humidity:** Medium. Mist weekly.
- **Light:** Bright, but out of direct sunlight.
- **Feeding:** Monthly, spring and summer.

General Care:
- Dislikes hot, dry air so fares better in non-centrally heated rooms.
- Can be trained around a frame or trellis.
- Suitable for indoor and outside hanging baskets.
- Wash leaves occasionally.

Troubleshooting:
- Brown tips on leaves; air is too dry.
- Loss of variegation; too dark.
- Older, mature leaves will naturally drop.

Pests & Diseases:
- Can be prone to red spider mite.

> **Trivia:**
> The purple-black berries produced by Hedera in the winter can be added into Christmas designs. They are also an important source of food for birds.

Family: Araliaceae.
Genus: Hedera.
Origin: Europe & Western Asia.

Hedera helix

Hibiscus

Common Name: Rose of China

Plant Notes: Pronounced 'Hi-BIS-skus.' A showy tropical flowering shrub which will provide weeks of large colourful blooms under the right conditions. Suitable for patios and containers in the warm summer months.

Type: Flowering houseplant.
Colour: All except for blue, green and purple.
Ideal Spot: Sunny windowsill or conservatory.
Height: Medium. 30cm/24".
Skill Level: Average.
Longevity: 5 + years.

Essential Care:
- **Temperature:** Cool to hot. 13–27°C/55–80°F.
- **Watering:** Evenly in summer, let compost dry out slightly in between.
- **Humidity:** Medium. Mist when in bud, stand in pebble tray.
- **Light:** Bright, shade from direct sun.
- **Feeding:** Weekly whilst in flower.

General Care:
- Will flower through the summer months.
- Individual flowers will only bloom for 2 to 3 days.
- Dislikes sudden changes in environment.

Troubleshooting:
- Loss of leaves; draughty or change in temperature.
- Bud drop; too dry or lack of humidity.

Pests & Diseases:
- Prone to aphids and red spider mite.

After Flowering:
Rest over winter in a minimum temperature of 15°C/60°F which will help buds to form. Water moderately and feed monthly. Prune back in spring.

Family: Malvaceae.
Genus: Hibiscus.
Origin: Temperate & tropical regions.

Hibiscus rosa-sinensis

Hippeastrum

Common Name: **Amaryllis**

Plant Notes: Pronounced 'Hippy-AST-strum.' Intrinsically linked to Christmas, these impressive flowering bulbs are hard to beat. Large trumpet shaped flowers top thick, leafless stems with sword shaped leaves rising from the base.

Type: Flowering bulb.
Colour: White, red, deep red, pink, peach.
Ideal Spot: Warm, bright room.
Height: Medium/tall. 90cm/36".
Skill Level: Easy.
Longevity: 5 + years.

Essential Care:
- **Temperature:** Cool/warm. 15–18°C/60–65°F.
- **Watering:** Weekly when in flower but avoid waterlogging compost.
- **Humidity:** Low. Not important.
- **Light:** Bright but avoid direct sunlight.
- **Feeding:** Weekly while in flower.

General Care:
- Blooms winter into spring.
- Top heavy when in flower, will need support.
- Turn pot occasionally as it will grow towards the light.
- Keep out of draughts and away from cold windowsills.

Troubleshooting:
- Green leaves but no flowers; bulb has not rested sufficiently.

Pests & Diseases:
- Relatively free from pests and diseases.

After Flowering:
Cut off the flower stalk, not the leaves. Place in a cool spot, watering and feeding sparingly during summer. In September remove old leaves and stop watering, allowing bulb to rest. Repot in fresh compost and bring into the warm in early December and resume watering and feeding.

Family: Amaryllidaceae.
Genus: Hippeastrum.
Origin: Central & South America.

Hippeastrum

Hoya

Common Name: Wax plant, Sweetheart Hoya

Plant Notes: Pronounced 'Hoy-uh.' An easy to grow fragrant climber or trailer with smooth, fleshy leaves. *H. carnosa* can be trained around a frame; *H. kerrii* has large, heart shaped leaves branching from a single stem.

Type: Succulent.
Colour: White flowers with pink centres.
Ideal Spot: Warm, sunny room.
Height: Mini to tall. 10–90cm/4–36".
Skill Level: Easy.
Longevity: 3 + years.

Essential Care:
- **Temperature:** Warm/hot. 15–27°C/60–80°F.
- **Watering:** With tepid water, allowing compost to dry out slightly.
- **Humidity:** Medium. Mist weekly, use pebble tray.
- **Light:** Bright but shade from direct sunlight.
- **Feeding:** Weekly, spring and summer.

Hoya kerrii

General Care:
- Flowers spring to autumn.
- Do not disturb once buds appear.
- Don't deadhead, as new flowers will form on old stalks.

Troubleshooting:
- Sudden loss of leaves; too wet or cold.
- Flower/bud drop; too dark.

Pests & Diseases:
- Mealy bugs and aphids.

After Flowering:
Feed monthly and water more sparingly between October and February. Needs a winter minimum temperature of 13°C/55°F. Prune only congested or spindly growth.

Family: Apocynaceae.
Genus: Hoya.
Origin: Eastern Asia & Australia.

Hoya carnosa

Hyacinthus

Common Name: **Hyacinth**

Plant Notes: Pronounced 'High-uh-cynth.' A fragrant spring flowering bulb, consisting of many bell-like florets covering a thick, fleshy stem. Often part of an indoor planted spring gift.

Type: Flowering bulb.
Colour: White, yellow, pink, red, blue, purple.
Ideal Spot: Sunny windowsill.

Height: Small. 25cm/10".
Skill Level: Easy.
Longevity: 2–4 weeks in flower.

Essential Care:
- **Temperature:** Cool/warm. 10–18°C/50–65°F.
- **Watering:** Just enough to keep compost damp.
- **Humidity:** Low. Not required.
- **Light:** Bright but avoid direct sunlight.
- **Feeding:** Feed after flowering if bulb is going to be planted outside afterwards.

General Care:
- Can become top heavy when in full flower.
- Be aware that planted bowls may not have any drainage.
- Can be an irritant, wear gloves when handling.
- Can be planted in the garden afterwards, see page 136.

Troubleshooting:
- Yellowing foliage; too wet, check that the compost isn't waterlogged.

Pests & Diseases:
- Relatively free from pests and diseases.

For Christmas Flowering:
Plant in moist bulb fibre in September with the tops of the bulbs just above the surface. Leave in a dark, cool place until flower tips emerge, (about eight weeks) then transfer to a lighter spot.

Family: Asparagaceae.
Genus: Hyacinth.
Origin: Eastern Mediterranean.

Hyacinthus orientalis

Hydrangea

Common Name: **Hydrangea**

Plant Notes: Pronounced 'Hi-drain-ja.' For a showy, indoor display, it's hard to beat the hydrangea with its large, impressive, spherical flower heads. They can be planted into the garden after flowering.

Type: Flowering houseplant.	**Height:** Medium. 60cm/24".
Colour: White, pink, purple, blue.	**Skill Level:** Easy.
Ideal Spot: Bright room or patio.	**Longevity:** 5 + years.

Essential Care:
- **Temperature:** Cool/warm. 10–18°C/50–65°F.
- **Watering:** Frequently in spring and summer, never allow roots to dry out.
- **Humidity:** Medium. Mist weekly.
- **Light:** Bright but shade from direct sunlight.
- **Feeding:** Every two weeks in growing season.

General Care:
- Use ericaceous compost for blue flowering hydrangea.
- Benefits from being immersed in water every now and then.
- Can go outside on a patio in the summer.
- Suitable for planting in the garden after flowering.

Troubleshooting:
- Wilting leaves; too dry, use immersion method.

Pests & Diseases:
- Botrytis, mildew, red spider mite, greenfly.

After Flowering:
Trim shoots back to about half their length to a pair of leaves. Overwinter in a frost-free room (minimum 13°C/55°F) and water sparingly. Bring into a warmer place in late winter and increase watering.

Family: Hydrangeaceae.
Genus: Hydrangea.
Origin: Eastern Asia & USA.

Hydrangea macrophylla

Hypoestes

Common Name: **Polka dot plant**

Plant Notes: Pronounced 'HIGH-po-es-tez.' A small, showy plant with brightly coloured mottled leaves. A lover of humidity, it makes excellent ground cover in terrariums. Has insignificant lavender flowers.

Type: Foliage houseplant.
Colour: Dark green; red, pink, cream blotches.
Ideal Spot: Terrarium, bathroom, kitchen.
Height: Small. 30cm/12".
Skill Level: Expert.
Longevity: 1–2 years.

Essential Care:
- **Temperature:** Warm/hot. 18–27°C/65–80°F.
- **Watering:** Use tepid water, keeping compost moist.
- **Humidity:** High. Mist every 2 to 3 days and use pebble tray.
- **Light:** Bright but avoid direct sunlight.
- **Feeding:** Weekly spring and summer.

General Care:
- Do not use leafshine and keep away from direct heat.
- Will become dormant after flowering, reduce watering and feed.
- Needs a winter minimum temperature of 13°C/55°F.
- Will quickly become leggy if not kept in shape by gentle pruning.

Troubleshooting:
- Drooping; too cold or overwatered.
- Crispy leaves; too dry.

Pests & Diseases:
- Powdery mildew.

Trivia:
Hypoestes make attractive trailing hanging basket plants if their growing tips are not pinched out. Spray frequently if basket is in full sun.

Family: Acanthaceae.
Genus: Hypoestes.
Origin: South Africa & Madagascar.

Hypoestes phyllostachya

Impatiens

Common Name: **Busy Lizzie**

Plant Notes:	Pronounced 'im-PAT-e-ons.' A cheerful flowering annual or perennial equally happy indoors or as part of an outdoor summer bedding scheme. Both single and double flowering, blooms can be plain or striped.
Type:	Flowering houseplant.
Colour:	White and all shades of pink, red and orange.
Ideal Spot:	Sunny windowsill, conservatory or patio.
Height:	Small. 30cm/12".
Skill Level:	Easy.
Longevity:	1–2 years.

Essential Care:
- **Temperature:** Warm. 13–18°C/55–65°F.
- **Watering:** Keep well-watered, but allow to dry out slightly in between.
- **Humidity:** Low. Mist occasionally.
- **Light:** As light as possible, but shaded from direct sunlight.
- **Feeding:** Weekly, spring and summer.

General Care:
- Pinch out the tips of young plants to keep them bushy.
- Avoid wetting flowers when misting or watering.
- Keeping it slightly pot bound will encourage flowering.

Troubleshooting:
- Loss of leaves; too cold or compost is too dry.
- Spindly growth; too warm or not enough light.

Pests & Diseases:
- Powdery mildew, whitefly, aphids, red spider mite.

> **Propagation:**
> At the end of summer, take stem cuttings from your plant, these will easily root in water. Once roots have developed, plant into potting compost, keep in a warm, bright spot. Discard original plant.

Family: Balsaminaceae.
Genus: Impatiens.
Origin: Eastern Africa.

Impatiens 'New Guinea' Group

Jasminum

Common Name: **Winter/Pink jasmine**

Plant Notes: Pronounced 'Jazz-MIN-e-um.' A wonderfully fragrant vigorous climbing plant with star-shaped flowers and attractive pinnate foliage. Can be easily trained along a hoop or onto trelliswork.

Type: Flowering climber.
Colour: Pure white with pink tinge.
Ideal Spot: Warm, sunny conservatory.
Height: Medium/tall. 75cm–3m/30"–10'.
Skill Level: Average.
Longevity: 5 + years.

Essential Care:
- **Temperature:** Warm/hot. 13–24°C/55–75°F.
- **Watering:** Weekly with tepid water spring to autumn.
- **Humidity:** Medium. Mist leaves frequently, avoiding wetting flowers.
- **Light:** Light as possible but shaded from direct sunlight.
- **Feeding:** Every two weeks spring to autumn.

General Care:
- Flowers late winter and early spring.
- Can take up to 10 years to reach maximum height.
- Can go outside in warm summer months.
- Will suffer in a centrally heated room.

Troubleshooting:
- Bud drop/brown buds; too hot or too dry.
- Buds not opening; needs more light.

Pests & Diseases:
- Red spider mite, greenfly.

After Flowering:
Cut back to half size, pinch out growing tips to encourage bushiness. Feed and water as normal until late autumn. Rest in a cool spot over winter (minimum 13°C/55°F) reduce watering. Bring back into warm conditions in January.

Family: Oleaceae.
Genus: Jasminum.
Origin: South-West China.

Jasminum polyanthum

Kalanchoe

Common Name: **Flaming Katy**

Plant Notes: Pronounced 'Ka-LAN-chi-oh.' One of the hardest working houseplants, Kalanchoe are cheerful, inexpensive and easy to keep, which goes a long way to explaining their popularity both commercially and in the home.

Type: Succulent.
Colour: White, yellow, orange, pink, red.
Ideal Spot: Any warm, sunny room.
Height: Mini/small. 30cm/12".
Skill Level: Easy.
Longevity: 1–2 years.

Essential Care:
- **Temperature:** Warm/hot. 13–23°C/55–75°F.
- **Watering:** Thoroughly but allow compost to dry out between.
- **Humidity:** Low. Mist occasionally if in a very warm room.
- **Light:** Bright, or semi-shade.
- **Feeding:** Weekly, spring and summer.

General Care:
- Water more sparingly in winter.
- Winter minimum temperature of 10°C/50°F.
- Move to a south-facing windowsill in winter.

Troubleshooting:
- Leaf drop; too wet, check for waterlogging.
- Black stems; too cold or wet.

Pests & Diseases:
- Relatively free from pests and diseases.

After Flowering:
Cut off the flowerheads and leave the plant to rest in a shady spot for approximately four to five weeks. Then move to a lighter spot and resume watering and feeding as before.

Family: Crassulaceae.
Genus: Kalanchoe.
Origin: Madagascar & Tropical Africa.

Kalanchoe blossfeldiana

Lithops

Common Name: **Living stone**

Plant Notes: Pronounced 'Lith-hops.' A fascinating plant with a pebble-like appearance which it has developed to mimic the conditions around it in its natural desert habitat. It produces tiny flowers in autumn.
Type: Succulent.
Colour: Mottled beige, brown, grey/green.
Ideal Spot: Warm sunny windowsill.
Height: Mini. 5cm/2".
Skill Level: Easy.
Longevity: 5 + years.

Essential Care:
- **Temperature:** Cool to hot. 5–30°C/41–86°F.
- **Watering:** Weekly spring to autumn, allow compost to dry out slightly in between.
- **Humidity:** Low. Not required.
- **Light:** Sunny, will tolerate all but the hottest sun.
- **Feeding:** Weekly, spring and summer.

General Care:
- Lithops need a shallow container with good drainage, can use cactus compost.
- They appreciate warm days and cool nights.
- Stop watering after flowering when the plant enters its dormant stage.
- Keep almost dry over autumn and winter.

Troubleshooting:
- Rotting at base; too wet, check for waterlogging and improve drainage.

Pests & Diseases:
- Relatively free from pests and diseases.

Trivia:
The mottled top surface of the plant is a 'leaf window' which allows light to enter, this is how the plant is able to carry out photosynthesis.

Family: Aizoaceae.
Genus: Lithops.
Origin: Southern Africa.

Lithops spp.

Livistona

Common Name: Chinese fan palm

Plant Notes: Pronounced 'Live-is-STONE-uh.' A slow growing, low maintenance specimen palm with toothed stalks which support elegant, almost circular fan shaped leaves.

CO_2

Type: Palm.
Colour: Mid-green.
Ideal Spot: Large living room or conservatory.
Height: Medium/tall. 1–2m/3–6'.
Skill Level: Easy.
Longevity: 10 + years.

Essential Care:
- **Temperature:** Warm. 15–21°C/60–70°F.
- **Watering:** Keep moist but not waterlogged.
- **Humidity:** Low. Mist with tepid water when in heated rooms.
- **Light:** Bright, or partial shade. Avoid direct sunlight.
- **Feeding:** Weekly in summer months only.

General Care:
- Reduce watering in winter.
- They need good drainage, never allow the plant to stand in water.
- It is natural for the lowest leaves to turn brown and drop.

Troubleshooting:
- Yellowing leaves; underwatering.
- Brown tip; air is too dry.
- Brown leaves; compost or root ball is too wet.

Pests & Diseases:
- Red spider mite, scale insects.

Trivia:
In 2011, after DNA testing, the genus *Livistona* was reclassified to *Saribus*. Rotundifolia is the Latin reference to its leaf shape.

Family: Arecaceae.
Genus: Saribus.
Origin: S/E Asia, Africa & Australia.

Saribus rotundifolius
Syn. *Livistona rotundifolia*

Mammillaria

Common Name: Pincushion cactus

Plant Notes: Pronounced 'MAM-mill-ar-re-uh.' A popular cactus and a great starter plant for children. It is one of the largest genera in the cactus family.

Type: Desert cactus.
Colour: Pink, yellow, red, white flowers.
Ideal Spot: Sunny windowsill.
Height: Mini/small. 4–30cm/2–12".
Skill Level: Easy.
Longevity: 10 + years.

Essential Care:
- **Temperature:** Cool to hot. 5–30°C/14–86°F.
- **Watering:** Weekly, through spring and summer.
- **Humidity:** Low. Not required but does like fresh air.
- **Light:** A light, sunny position, shade from full sun.
- **Feeding:** Every three weeks, spring to autumn.

General Care:
- Use cactus compost and let it dry out slightly between watering.
- Water sparingly in autumn and winter, keeping it almost dry.
- Needs a bright, sunny, cool position in winter.

Troubleshooting:
- Base rot; overwatering, especially in winter months.

Pests & Diseases:
- Mealy bugs, red spider mite, scale insects.

Flowering:
Most cactus will bloom annually once they have reached maturity, for Mammillaria this is between 3 to 4 years. A winter resting period is important to encourage flowering, they also prefer to be slightly pot bound.

Family: Cactaceae.
Genus: Mammillaria.
Origin: Mexico.

Mammillaria spp.

Maranta

Common Name: **Prayer plant**

Plant Notes: Pronounced 'Ma-RAN-tah.' A striking plant whose soft, paddle shaped leaves have distinctive, artistically marked foliage with strongly coloured veins and contrasting patches.

Type: Foliage houseplant.
Colour: Deep/light green, burgundy, red, cream.
Ideal Spot: Warm, humid room.
Height: Medium. 60cm/24".
Skill Level: Expert.
Longevity: 3–4 years.

Essential Care:
- **Temperature:** Warm. 18–21°C/65–70°F.
- **Watering:** Soft, tepid water, always keep compost moist.
- **Humidity:** High. Mist every 2 to 3 days, stand in pebble tray.
- **Light:** Partial shade; leaf colour will fade in direct sunlight.
- **Feeding:** Every two weeks spring and summer.

General Care:
- Needs a warm, draught free, shady spot.
- Don't use leafshine, clean leaves with a damp cloth.
- Avoid draughts and sudden changes in temperature.

Troubleshooting:
- Brown leaf tips/leaf fall; air is too dry.
- Leaves curled and yellowing; underwatering.

Pests & Diseases:
- Red spider mite.

> **Trivia:**
> In their natural habitat Maranta grow under the tree canopy of the tropical rain forest, hence its need for a warm, humid atmosphere.

Family: Marantaceae.
Genus: Maranta.
Origin: Tropical South America.

Maranta tricolour

Medinilla

Common Name: **Rose grape**

Plant Notes: Pronounced 'MED-in-nil-uh.' A spectacular tropical flowering houseplant with pendulous, grape like flowers hanging from shell pink bracts. Not a plant for the fainthearted!

Type: Flowering houseplant.
Colour: Rose pink.
Ideal Spot: Large warm conservatory or greenhouse.
Height: Tall. 90cm/36".
Skill Level: Expert.
Longevity: 1–2 years.

Essential Care:
- **Temperature:** Warm/hot. 18–27°C/64–80°F.
- **Watering:** Weekly from below, spring and summer. Allow to dry out slightly in between.
- **Humidity:** High. Mist daily and stand in pebble tray.
- **Light:** Bright but avoid direct sunlight.
- **Feeding:** Every two weeks March to September.

General Care:
- Flowers in spring and early summer.
- Humidity and warmth must be kept constant.
- Use orchid compost and distilled or rainwater if possible.
- Deadhead regularly.

Troubleshooting:
- Bud drop; not enough light or compost/air too dry.
- Leaves wilting; exposure to draughts or overwatering.

Pests & Diseases:
- Red spider mite.

After Flowering:
To stop it becoming leggy, cut stems back to a pair of leaves. Continue feeding but reduce watering. In winter stop feeding, water sparingly to allow the plant to rest. Maintain warmth and humidity.

Family: Melastomataceae.
Genus: Medinilla.
Origin: Philippines.

Medinilla magnifica

Microsorum

Common Name: Crocodile fern, Java fern

Plant Notes: Pronounced 'my-kroh-SOR-um.' An interesting fern with distinctive crinkly leaves. It varies widely in size and leaf shape depending on its environment.

Type: Fern.
Colour: Bright glossy green.
Ideal Spot: Warm, humid spot.
Height: Medium. 60cm/24".
Skill Level: Easy.
Longevity: 5 + years.

Essential Care:
- **Temperature:** Warm. 15–21°C/60–70°F.
- **Watering:** Keep moist, letting compost dry out slightly in between.
- **Humidity:** Medium. Mist weekly, use pebble tray.
- **Light:** Indirect light shade.
- **Feeding:** Monthly, spring and summer.

General Care:
- Water sparingly in winter.
- Keep out of draughts and away from direct heat.
- Suitable for hanging baskets.

Troubleshooting:
- Soft, wilting leaves; either too cold or overwatering.

Pests & Diseases:
- Relatively free from pests and diseases.

Trivia:
Microsorums grow from rhizomes and there are over 50 species which can be found in warm tropical areas ranging from New Zealand to China.

Family: Polypodiaceae.
Genus: Microsorum.
Origin: Tropical regions of Southern hemisphere.

Microsorum pteropus

Monstera

Common Name: **Swiss cheese plant**

Plant Notes: Pronounced 'Mon-STEER-rah.' One of the most recognisable of all houseplants, this impressive specimen with its deeply cut leaves is best reserved for a large, airy space where it can grow to its full potential.

Type: Foliage houseplant.
Colour: Dark glossy green.
Ideal Spot: Large, light room.

Height: Tall. 2.5m/10'.
Skill Level: Easy.
Longevity: 10 + years.

Essential Care:
- **Temperature:** Warm/hot. 18–24°C/65–75°F.
- **Watering:** Water frequently in summer, avoid waterlogging.
- **Humidity:** Medium. Mist weekly, spring and summer.
- **Light:** Bright, but out of direct sunlight.
- **Feeding:** Monthly spring to autumn.

General Care:
- Use a moss pole to give support.
- The leaves divide as they mature.
- Wash leaves occasionally with a damp cloth but avoid handling new growth.
- Reduce watering in winter.

Troubleshooting:
- Yellowing leaves; overwatering, especially in winter.
- Brown edges and tips; air or compost is too dry.

Pests & Diseases:
- Red spider mite.

Trivia:
Monstera produce aerial roots which operate in the same way as roots underground. To stop them drying out, push them back into compost or tie them carefully onto the supporting moss pole.

Family: Araceae.
Genus: Monstera.
Origin: Mexico & Central America.

Monstera deliciosa

Muehlenbeckia

Common Name: **Maidenhair vine, Wire vine**

Plant Notes: Pronounced 'Mule-en-BECK-e-uh.' A vigorous semi-deciduous vine which in its natural environment grows as a dense, wiry ground covering mat. It will grow around a frame, or trail from a hanging basket.

Type: Foliage houseplant.
Colour: Dark to mid green.
Ideal Spot: Shady windowsill or porch.
Trails: 90cm/36".
Skill Level: Easy.
Longevity: 5 + years.

Essential Care:
- **Temperature:** Cool/warm. 10–15°C/50–60°F.
- **Watering:** Keep compost moist but not over wet.
- **Humidity:** Low. Mist occasionally if in a centrally heated room.
- **Light:** A light, semi-shaded spot is ideal.
- **Feeding:** Every two weeks in spring.

General Care:
- Needs good drainage, don't let it sit in water.
- Newly bought plants don't need to be fed for the first year.
- It will naturally loose some of its leaves in winter.
- Rest in winter, reduce watering and move to a cool spot, minimum of 1°C/34°F.

Troubleshooting:
- Leaf drop; compost is too dry.

Pests & Diseases:
- Relatively free from pests and diseases.

In Design Use:
Strands can be carefully cut from the plant and used in modern designs for caging, winding or veiling. With trails of up to and over 30cm it is very versatile.

Family: Polygonaceae.
Genus: Muehlenbeckia.
Origin: New Zealand & Pacific borders.

Muehlenbeckia complexa

Musa

Common Name: Banana plant

Plant Notes: Pronounced 'Moo-sah.' Add a touch of the tropical to your houseplant collection, although you will need a lot of space! Treat as a decorative specimen, it is unlikely to produce fruit.

Type: Foliage houseplant.
Colour: Bright green.
Ideal Spot: Large conservatory or greenhouse.
Height: Tall. 120cm/4'.
Skill Level: Average.
Longevity: 5 + years.

Essential Care:
- **Temperature:** Warm/hot. 18–24°C/65–75°F.
- **Watering:** Frequently to keep compost moist, but don't let it stand in water.
- **Humidity:** Medium. Mist weekly, but not when in full sun.
- **Light:** Bright, with some direct sun.
- **Feeding:** Weekly, spring to summer.

General Care:
- Don't let leaves touch windows in hot weather.
- Yellowing of lower leaves is normal.
- The large, delicate leaves damage easily, handle with care.
- Requires a minimum all year temperature of 15°C/60°F.

Troubleshooting:
- Wilting and yellowing leaves; underwatering, the root ball should never be left to dry out.
- Brown tips on leaves; sun scorch.

Pests & Diseases:
- Red spider mite.

Winter Care:
Reduce watering, but not to the extent that the plant dries out. Stop feeding and rest in a warm, bright spot. Resume normal watering and feeding in spring. Not frost hardy.

Family: Musaceae.
Genus: Musa.
Origin: South-East Asia.

Musa 'Tropicana'

Narcissus

Common Name: **Daffodil**

Plant Notes: Pronounced 'NAR-sis-us.' A pot of flowering narcissus is the perfect way to bring a touch of spring into the house. Paperwhite and Tête-à-tête varieties will provide both flowers and scent over the Christmas and New Year period.

Type: Flowering bulb.
Colour: Yellow, white, with contrasting centres.
Ideal Spot: Warm, bright room.
Height: Small. 30cm/12".
Skill Level: Easy.
Longevity: 2–3 weeks in flower.

Essential Care:
- **Temperature:** Cool/warm. 15–21°C/60–70°F.
- **Watering:** Water with care, keeping compost on the dry side.
- **Humidity:** Low. Not required.
- **Light:** Bright, away from direct sunlight.
- **Feeding:** Every two weeks after flowering has finished.

General Care:
- Seasonal, flowering late winter and spring.
- Keep in a cool spot until flower buds emerge, then move into a warmer place.
- Avoid placing in draughts or near direct sources of heat.
- Can be planted in the garden in autumn.

Troubleshooting:
- Yellowing foliage or brown flowers/buds; too wet.

Pests & Diseases:
- Relatively free from pests and diseases.

After Flowering:
Cut off flower stalks but not leaves and water with a weak solution of feed until the leaves wither. Take the bulbs out of the pot and store them in a cool, dry place until autumn, then replant.

Family: Amaryllidaceae.
Genus: Narcissus.
Origin: Europe & Asia.

Narcissus Tête-à-tête

Neoregelia

Common Name: **Blushing Bromeliad**

Plant Notes: Pronounced 'nee-o-reg-EL-e-uh'. One of the most vibrant plants in the Bromeliad family with leathery leaves arching from a central vase. They are epiphytic by nature.

Type: Bromeliad.
Colour: Green/cream; vibrant pink, red.
Ideal Spot: Sunny windowsill.
Height: Medium. 60cm/24".
Skill Level: Average.
Longevity: 1–2 years.

Essential Care:

- **Temperature:** Warm/hot. 18–27°C/65–80°F.
- **Watering:** With rainwater in central vase, which should be refreshed regularly.
- **Humidity:** Medium. Mist with tepid water in hot months.
- **Light:** Needs a bright spot, will tolerate some direct sunlight.
- **Feeding:** Weekly, spring and summer.

General Care:

- Also keep compost moist, allowing it to dry out slightly in between watering.
- Stop feeding and water more sparingly in winter.
- Has a shallow root system, needs a small pot.

Troubleshooting:

- Plant rot; overwatering.
- Colour fading on leaves; not enough light.

Pests & Diseases:

- Relatively free from pests and diseases.

Trivia:
Neoregelia are at their most colourful when coming into flower and remain so for several months. The plant will produce plantlets on stolons which can be removed and potted on.

Family: Bromeliaceae.
Genus: Neoregelia.
Origin: Brazilian rainforests.

Neoregelia carolinae

Nepenthes

Common Name: **Monkey cups**

Plant Notes: Pronounced 'Na-PEN-thez.' A fascinating member of the carnivorous plant family with pendent, jug shaped traps designed to trap and devour passing insects. Suitable for hanging baskets.

Type: Carnivorous.
Colour: Green with red, brown, orange pitchers.
Ideal Spot: Any bright, sunny room.
Height: Medium. 30cm/24".
Skill Level: Expert.
Longevity: 2 + years.

Essential Care:
- **Temperature:** Warm/hot. 15–25°C/60–75°F.
- **Watering:** With distilled or rainwater, keep compost moist but not wet.
- **Humidity:** High. Constant humidity is important, mist weekly.
- **Light:** Direct or partial sunlight, but shade from hot sun through glass.
- **Feeding:** Spray with diluted orchid feed every two weeks, spring to summer.

General Care:
- Protect from draughts, extreme heat and freezing temperatures.
- Use specialist carnivorous or orchid compost.
- Can add dried crickets and flies to the cups, don't overfeed.
- Appreciates cooler night temperatures of 15°C/60°F.

Troubleshooting:
- Weak growth and lack of colour; not enough light.
- Cups failing to develop; not humid enough.
- Cups turning black; overfeeding.

Pests & Diseases:
- Relatively free from pests and diseases.

Nepenthes

Trivia:
Known as Monkey cups as, in their natural environment, monkeys drink rainwater from them.

Family: Nepenthaceae.
Genus: Nepenthes.
Origin: Old World Tropics.

Nephrolepis

Common Name: Boston fern, Sword fern

Plant Notes: Pronounced 'Neph-FRO-lep-is.' An elegant, graceful fern popular since the Victorian times, with sword shaped leaves and distinctive herringbone foliage. A lovely specimen plant for home or office.

Type:	Fern.	**Height:**	Medium/tall. 90cm/36".
Colour:	Fresh, bright green.	**Skill Level:**	Average.
Ideal Spot:	Bright, humid spot.	**Longevity:**	5 + years.

Essential Care:
- **Temperature:** Warm. 13–18°C/55–65°F.
- **Watering:** 2 to 3 times a week with tepid water.
- **Humidity:** High. Mist daily with tepid water, use pebble tray.
- **Light:** Bright to semi-shade. Keep out of direct sunlight.
- **Feeding:** Weekly, spring and summer.

General Care:
- Compost should always be moist, but not waterlogged.
- Keep away from draughts and direct heat sources.
- If looking straggly, can be cut back to just above compost level where it will regrow.
- Avoid using leafshine or insecticides.
- Water more sparingly in winter.

Troubleshooting:
- Leaf drop; air is too dry, increase humidity.

Pests & Diseases:
- Scale insects, red spider mite.

> **Propagation:**
> Small plantlets will form on runners that emerge from the crown of the plant. These can be removed and potted into a peaty mixture. Keep warm, 20°C/68°F, for the new plants to establish.

Family: Lomariopsidaceae.
Genus: Nephrolepis.
Origin: Tropical regions.

Nephrolepis exaltata

Nertera

Common Name: Bead plant, Pincushion plant

Plant Notes: Pronounced 'Ner-TER-ra.' The tiny leaves of this ground cover plant are almost obscured by the mass of brightly coloured spherical berries which appear in autumn. Bears tiny white/green flowers in summer.

Type: Decorative houseplant.
Colour: Bright green with orange berries.
Ideal Spot: Bright, warm windowsill.
Height: Small. 15cm/6".
Skill Level: Expert.
Longevity: 1 year.

Essential Care:
- **Temperature:** Cool/warm. 13–18°C/55–65°F.
- **Watering:** Keep compost moist, always water from below.
- **Humidity:** Medium. Mist weekly, use pebble tray.
- **Light:** Bright, minimum 3 to 4 hours a day, shade from direct sun.
- **Feeding:** Once a month as berries start to appear.

General Care:
- Allow the plant to dry out slightly in between watering.
- Likes fresh air, can go outside in summer.
- Difficult to overwinter, often discarded after berries have finished.

Troubleshooting:
- A straggly plant with no berries; too dark or too warm.

Pests & Diseases:
- Relatively free from pests and diseases.

Winter Care:
Nertera grows at high altitudes in its natural habitat, so choose a cool, sunny spot, with a winter minimum temperature of 7°C/45°F. Reduce watering and stop feeding.

Family: Rubiaceae.
Genus: Nertera.
Origin: Southern hemisphere.

Nertera granadensis

Oncidium

Common Name: **Butterfly orchid**

Plant Notes: Pronounced 'On-SID-ee-um.' Sometimes called a spray orchid, this is a delicate plant with relatively small, pretty flowers. The arching, slender stems can be cut and used in bridal work.

Type: Orchid.
Colour: Green, sulphur yellow, red, orange.
Ideal Spot: Warm, bright windowsill.

Height: Medium. 60cm/24".
Skill Level: Average.
Longevity: 5 + years.

Essential Care:
- **Temperature:** Warm/hot. 18–24°C/65–75°F.
- **Watering:** Keep compost moist with soft tepid rainwater.
- **Humidity:** Medium. Mist air around the plant and stand in pebble tray.
- **Light:** Needs lots of light, 10 to 15 hours a day, avoid direct sun.
- **Feeding:** Once a month with orchid fertilizer.

General Care:
- Needs a difference between day and night temperature.
- Avoid moving the plant once it is settled.
- Use orchid compost and don't let the plant sit in water.
- Avoid wetting the flowers and leaves when misting.

Troubleshooting:
- Dark green leaves; not enough light.

Pests & Diseases:
- Relatively free from pests and diseases.

After Flowering:
Stop feeding and reduce watering, keep in a cool place, minimum temperature of 15°C/60°F, for approximately two months. Increase watering and resume feeding when new a shoot appears.

Family: Orchidaceae.
Genus: Oncidium.
Origin: South & Central America.

Oncidium

Opuntia

Common Name: Bunny ears cactus, Prickly pear

Plant Notes: Pronounced 'Oh-PUN-tee-uh.' This cactus belongs to a huge genera with some desert species growing up to 7m/23'. Unmistakable flattened pads are covered with groups of sharp bristles. It produces flowers in spring and summer.

Type: Desert cactus.
Height: Mini to medium. 10–60cm/4–24".
Colour: Sage green; white and pink flowers.
Skill Level: Easy.
Ideal Spot: Warm, sunny windowsill.
Longevity: 5 + years.

Essential Care:
- **Temperature:** Warm/hot. 5–27°C/41–80°F.
- **Watering:** Thoroughly spring and summer allow to dry out slightly in between.
- **Humidity:** Low. Misting not required but likes fresh air.
- **Light:** Bright, sunny spot, will tolerate some direct sun.
- **Feeding:** In summer only, every 3 to 4 weeks.

General Care:
- Use specialist cactus feed and compost.
- Provide ventilation by opening a window on hot days.
- Needs winter sun, but don't leave it on a cold windowsill at night.
- Opuntia will only bloom when the plant is mature.

Troubleshooting:
- Shrivelled or rotting; overwatering in winter.
- Lack of growth; compost is either too wet or too dry.

Pests & Diseases:
- Red spider mite, mealy bugs.

> **Winter Care:**
> They need a cool, dry, dormant period but with plenty of light. Water sparingly November to February. Move into a warmer spot in early spring, increase watering and start feeding.

Family: Cactaceae.
Genus: Opuntia.
Origin: The Americas.

Opuntia microdasys

Paphiopedilum

Common Name: Slipper orchid, Venus slipper orchid

Plant Notes: Pronounced 'Path-e-o-PED-e-lum.' A striking orchid which produces an impressive single flower with spotted and striped markings and a bulbous lower lip. Some also have attractive mottled leaves.

Type: Orchid.
Colour: Green, tan, yellow, white.
Ideal Spot: East facing windowsill.
Height: Small. 30cm/12".
Skill Level: Average.
Longevity: Flowers 3–6 months.

Essential Care:
- **Temperature:** Cool/warm. 10–24°C/50–75°F.
- **Watering:** Water from below spring to autumn with distilled water, keep compost moist.
- **Humidity:** High. Mist air around the plant and in pebble tray.
- **Light:** Filtered light with shade from direct sun.
- **Feeding:** Every 2 to 3 weeks spring to autumn.

General Care:
- Flowering period November to March.
- Plants with mottled leaves can be kept at slightly higher temperatures.
- They appreciate an occasional blast of fresh air.
- Use specialised orchid compost and food.

Troubleshooting:
- Brown flower buds; usually caused by cold draughts.

Pests & Diseases:
- Aphids, scale insects, whitefly, red spider mite, mealy bugs.

After Flowering:
Repot between February and June in a pot just large enough to accommodate the roots. Any off-shoots can be carefully removed and potted on.

Family: Orchidaceae.
Genus: Paphiopedilum.
Origin: Far East.

Paphiopedilum

Passiflora

Common Name: **Passion flower**

Plant Notes: Pronounced 'PASS-e-floor-uh.' A vigorous, tropical evergreen climber with distinctive bowl-shaped flowers and deeply lobed foliage. Produces orange fruits which are only edible when mature.

Type: Flowering climber.
Colour: White, purple, blue.
Ideal Spot: Large conservatory or patio.
Height: Tall. 90cm/36".
Skill Level: Expert.
Longevity: 10 + years.

Essential Care:
- **Temperature:** Warm/hot. 13–24°C/55–75°F.
- **Watering:** Weekly in summer, keeping compost moist.
- **Humidity:** Medium. Mist weekly, stand on pebble tray.
- **Light:** Bright, 3 to 4 hours of indirect light a day.
- **Feeding:** Weekly during summer months.

General Care:
- Flowers May to November; frost hardy.
- Needs good ventilation, can go outside in summer.
- Able to be trained onto a hoop or trellis.
- Keeping it pot bound encourages flowering.

Troubleshooting:
- No flowers; not enough bright light.
- Healthy foliage but no flowers; overfeeding.

Pests & Diseases:
- Aphids, whitefly, red spider mite, mealy bugs.

Winter Care:
After flowering, reduce watering to every two weeks and stop feeding. Rest in a cool spot with a winter minimum temperature of 7°C/45°F. Prune back straggly growth in early spring.

Family: Passifloraceae.
Genus: Passiflora.
Origin: South America.

Passiflora caerulea

Pellaea

Common Name: **Button fern**

Plant Notes: Pronounced 'Pe-LEE-ah.' A small, compact fern with shiny leaflets growing in pairs along arched wiry stalks. The leaves, round at first, become oval as they mature.

Type: Fern.
Colour: Dark green.
Ideal Spot: Bright windowsill.
Height: Small. 20cm/8".
Skill Level: Easy.
Longevity: 2 + years.

Essential Care:
- **Temperature:** Warm. 13–18°C/55–65°F.
- **Watering:** Keep compost constantly moist, but not wet.
- **Humidity:** Medium. Mist weekly, stand on pebble tray.
- **Light:** Indirect, will tolerate some shade, avoid direct sun.
- **Feeding:** Monthly spring to autumn.

General Care:
- Acid loving, use ericaceous compost.
- Likes fresh air, can go outside in summer.
- Needs good drainage, don't allow plant to sit in water.
- Reduce watering in winter and allow plant to rest.

Troubleshooting:
- Plant collapse; compost is too wet.

Pests & Diseases:
- Scale insects, mealy bugs, aphids.

Trivia:
Its name is from the Greek 'pellos' meaning dark-coloured or dusky, a reference to the colour of the stems.

Family: Pteridaceae.
Genus: Pellaea.
Origin: New Zealand.

Pellaea rotundifolia

Peperomia

Common Name: **Radiator plant**

Plant Notes: Pronounced 'Pepper-ROW-me-uh.' The textured, richly coloured leaves of the Peperomia are the main attraction of this easy to care for plant. Some produce slim, tail-like creamy flower spikes.

Type: Foliage houseplant.
Colour: Shades of green, purple and pink.
Ideal Spot: Bathroom or kitchen.
Height: Small. 25cm/10".
Skill Level: Easy.
Longevity: 2 – 3 years.

Essential Care:
- **Temperature:** Warm. 13–18°C/55–65°F.
- **Watering:** Use tepid water, allowing compost to dry out slightly in between.
- **Humidity:** Low. Mist air around plant.
- **Light:** Indirect light or semi-shade. Protect from direct sun.
- **Feeding:** Every two weeks spring to autumn.

General Care:
- Don't overwater as they store moisture in their leaves.
- Smaller varieties are suitable for dish gardens.
- Trailing types can go into hanging baskets.

Troubleshooting:
- Brown edges on leaves; too draughty.
- Leaf drop in winter; too cold.
- Wilted/discoloured leaves; overwatering.

Pests & Diseases:
- Red spider mite.

> **Trivia:**
> There are over 1,000 species of this compact, slow growing plant. Some are upright, some bushy and some trailing but are all mainly concentrated in Central and South America.

Family: Piperaceae.
Genus: Peperomia.
Origin: Tropical America.

Peperomia caperata

Pericallis

Common Name: Cineraria, Senecio

Plant Notes: Pronounced 'Pe-ree-CAL-is.' A bright and cheerful free-flowering annual which produces vividly coloured daisy-like flowers above a mass of soft, triangular shaped leaves.
Type: Flowering houseplant.
Colour: Magenta, blue, violet, also bi-coloured.
Ideal Spot: Cool, with indirect light.
Height: Small. 30cm/12".
Skill Level: Average.
Longevity: Annual.

Essential Care:
- **Temperature:** Cool/warm. 10–21°C/55–70°F.
- **Watering:** Keep compost moist but not wet, using tepid water.
- **Humidity:** Low. Use pebble tray, avoid wetting leaves and flowers.
- **Light:** Bright, indirect light, never in full sun.
- **Feeding:** Monthly, spring to autumn.

General Care:
- Flowers during spring and summer.
- Keep away from draughts but provide some air circulation.
- Never let the compost become waterlogged.
- After the final flowering period, discard or recycle.

Troubleshooting:
- Plant collapse; either too hot, or compost is too wet.
- Yellowing leaves and wilting foliage; underwatering or in a draught.

Pests & Diseases:
- Aphids, whitefly, botrytis.

After Flowering:
When the first flush of flowers has died, cut the stems back to 10–15cm/4–6". This will encourage a second burst of flowers. Recycle at the end of autumn.

Family: Asteraceae.
Genus: Pericallis.
Origin: Canary Islands.

Pericallis x hybrida
Syn. *Senecio cruentus*

Phalaenopsis

Common Name: **Moth orchid**

Plant Notes: Pronounced 'Fal-en-OP-sis.' One of the best-selling orchids and it's easy to see why, with its delicate arching stems and attractive, long-lasting bi-coloured, spotted or striped blooms.

Type: Orchid.
Colour: White, pink, purple, yellow, lime.
Ideal Spot: East or west facing windowsill.
Height: Medium. 60cm/24".
Skill Level: Average.
Longevity: 3 + years.

Essential Care:
- **Temperature:** Warm/hot. Day: 27°C/80°F. Night: 18°C/65°F.
- **Watering:** Keep compost moist, water from below.
- **Humidity:** Medium. Mist weekly, use pebble tray.
- **Light:** Bright, indirect light, 10 to 12 hours a day.
- **Feeding:** Every 7 to 10 days with specialised feed.

General Care:
- Water in the morning with distilled water.
- Don't let the plant sit in water.
- Needs good ventilation but avoid draughts.
- Needs a difference in day and night temperatures.

Troubleshooting:
- Drooping, floppy leaves; lack of light.
- Dark red pigmentation on leaves; too dark.
- Crown rot; caused by water standing in centre of plant.

Pests & Diseases:
- Relatively free from pests and diseases.

After Flowering:
Cut back green spike to nearest node. If spike doesn't re-flower and turns brown, cut off at base. Let the plant rest, feed monthly and reduce watering with a night temperature of a cool 10°C/55°F. Move into a warmer spot once new spike appears, resume watering and feeding as before.

Family: Orchidaceae.
Genus: Phalaenopsis.
Origin: Tropical Asia.

Phalaenopsis

Philodendron

Common Name: **Sweetheart plant**

Plant Notes: Pronounced 'PHIL-oh-den-dron.' Popular since Victorian times, the impressive climbing types will need space and a moss pole for support. Non-climbing, tree Philodendrons also need plenty of room to spread.

Type: Foliage houseplant.
Colour: Rich glossy green, reddish brown.
Ideal Spot: Large sunny room.
Height: Tall. 2m/6'.
Skill Level: Easy.
Longevity: 10 + years.

Essential Care:
- **Temperature:** Warm/hot. 15–21°C/60–70°F.
- **Watering:** Thoroughly in spring and summer.
- **Humidity:** Medium. Keep air around plant moist, use pebble tray.
- **Light:** Semi-shade, out of direct sunlight.
- **Feeding:** Weekly in summer, increasing doses as plant grows.

General Care:
- Allow the plant to dry out slightly in between watering.
- Needs a cooler winter temperature of 12–18°C/53–65°F.
- Reduce feeding in winter to every 2 to 3 weeks.
- Prune back in late winter.

Troubleshooting:
- Yellowing leaves; over or underwatering.
- Leggy growth; too much shade.
- Leaves with brown edges or tips; air too dry.

Pests & Diseases:
- Mealy bugs.

Trivia:
The plants aerial roots should be pushed carefully back into the compost or moss pole as they provide moisture and food for the upper leaves as the plant grows.

Family: Araceae.
Genus: Philodendron.
Origin: Tropical America.

Philodendron scandens

Phoenix

Common Name: **Date palm**

Plant Notes: Pronounced 'FEE-nix.' A quick growing palm with spikey stiff leaflets rising from a thick, fibrous stem. A popular specimen plant often found in office landscaping schemes.

Type: Palm.
Colour: Dark green.
Ideal Spot: Large conservatory or sunny room.
Height: Tall. 2m/6'.
Skill Level: Easy.
Longevity: 10 + years.

Essential Care:
- **Temperature:** Warm/hot. 15–21°C/60–70°F.
- **Watering:** Tepid water, keeping compost moist, but not waterlogged.
- **Humidity:** High. Mist every few days with tepid water.
- **Light:** Bright sunny spot, will tolerate some direct sun.
- **Feeding:** Weekly in summer, every 2 to 3 weeks in winter.

General Care:
- Very sensitive to changes in the environment.
- Avoid cleaning leaves with leafshine, use a damp cloth.
- Likes fresh air, can go outside in summer.

Troubleshooting:
- Leaves yellow or with brown tips; underwatering.
- Leaves with brown spots; exposure to draughts.

Pests & Diseases:
- Red spider mite, scale insects.

Trivia:
The fruits of *Phoenix canariensis* are edible but small and thin skinned. It is *P. dactylifera* which produces the sugar rich pulpy fruit which is eaten worldwide.

Family: Arecaceae.
Genus: Phoenix.
Origin: Canary Islands & Middle East.

Phoenix canariensis

Pilea

Common Name: Aluminium plant

Plant Notes: Pronounced 'Pie-LEE-a.' A hard-working plant that comes in many forms, bushy, creeping and trailing. It is suitable for hanging baskets and can go outside in summer months. It is a member of the nettle family.

Type: Foliage houseplant.
Colour: Green; silver, burgundy markings.
Ideal Spot: Warm room, shaded from direct sun.
Height: Small. 15cm/6".
Skill Level: Easy.
Longevity: 3 + years.

Essential Care:
- **Temperature:** Warm/hot. 15–21°C/60–70°F.
- **Watering:** Liberally spring to autumn with tepid water.
- **Humidity:** Medium. Mist weekly.
- **Light:** Semi-shade, protect from direct sun.
- **Feeding:** Every two weeks, spring to autumn.

General Care:
- Avoid draughts and cold windowsills.
- Let compost dry out slightly in between watering.
- Not frost tolerant.

Pilea involucrata

Troubleshooting:
- Leaf fall; too cold or wet, cut back affected stems.
- Wilting leaves; stem rot, too wet.
- Brown tips on leaves; too dark.

Pests & Diseases:
- Red spider mite, mealy bugs, botrytis.

Winter Care:
Reduce watering and stop feeding, remove dead leaves and pinch out growing tips to keep plant bushy. Trim in spring, if it becomes leggy – recycle.

Family: Utricaceae.
Genus: Pilea.
Origin: Warm temperate regions.

Pilea cadierei

Platycerium

Common Name: Staghorn fern, Elkhorn fern

Plant Notes: Pronounced 'Plait-e-SEE-re-um.' A fascinating fern with an antler-like appearance, hence the common name. The thick, leathery leaves are covered with a soft, waxy, white down.

Type: Fern.
Colour: Sage green.
Ideal Spot: Hanging basket out of direct sun.
Height: Medium/tall. 90cm/36".
Skill Level: Average.
Longevity: 5 + years.

Essential Care:
- **Temperature:** Warm/hot. 15–24°C/60–75°F.
- **Watering:** Use immersion method and soft water, keep compost moist.
- **Humidity:** High. Mist daily, but don't allow fronds to become damp.
- **Light:** Bright, filtered light.
- **Feeding:** Once a month spring to autumn.

General Care:
- Don't sponge the leaves or use leafshine.
- Can use orchid compost. Reduce watering in winter.
- Brown, papery leaves are natural and normal.

Troubleshooting:
- Yellowing tips on fronds; too warm or dry.

Pests & Diseases:
- Scale insects.

> **Trivia:**
> This fascinating fern has both fertile and sterile leaves. Its base, or anchor leaves, are used in its natural habitat to attach itself to tree trunks.

> **Family:** Polypodiaceae.
> **Genus:** Platycerium.
> **Origin:** Tropical regions.

Platycerium bifurcatum

Pteris

Common Name: Ladder fern, Brake fern

Plant Notes: Pronounced 'TARE-iss.' With pretty, delicate fronds the Pteris is very much a traditional fern. Capable of growing up to 60cm/24" although it is usually the smaller varieties that are most popular for the home.

Type: Fern.
Colour: Mid/bright green, silver markings.
Ideal Spot: Warm, shady room.
Height: Small. 20cm/8".
Skill Level: Easy.
Longevity: 3 + years.

Essential Care:
- **Temperature:** Warm/hot. 13–24°C/55–75°F.
- **Watering:** Keep compost moist, but not waterlogged.
- **Humidity:** High. Mist every 2 to 3 days use pebble tray.
- **Light:** Semi-shade, avoiding strong sunlight.
- **Feeding:** Monthly, spring to autumn.

General Care:
- Avoid draughts and sudden changes in temperature.
- Appreciates a difference between day and night temperatures.
- Reduce watering and stop feeding in winter.
- Clean out old leaves from the centre of the plant in autumn.

Troubleshooting:
- Plant collapse; too wet.
- Ends of leaves turning brown; air too dry.

Pests & Diseases:
- Relatively free from pests and diseases.

Trivia:
The common name, Brake, is derived from Old English 'bracu' or thicket. A 'fearnbraca' was a thicket of ferns.

Family: Pteridaceae.
Genus: Pteris.
Origin: Tropical & sub-tropical regions.

Pteris cretica

Radermachera

Common Name: China doll plant

Plant Notes: Pronounced 'Rad-er-MOK-er-uh.' A fairly new houseplant introduced from Taiwan in the 1980's, with glossy evergreen leaves divided into leaflets and a sturdy, tree-like growth.

Type: Foliage houseplant.
Colour: Deep green.
Ideal Spot: Any bright, warm room.
Height: Medium/tall. 90cm/36".
Skill Level: Easy.
Longevity: 5 + years.

Essential Care:
- **Temperature:** Warm/hot. 18–24°C/65–75°F.
- **Watering:** Keep compost moist but not waterlogged.
- **Humidity:** Low. Mist occasionally.
- **Light:** Bright, 4 to 5 hours a day, protect from direct sun.
- **Feeding:** Every 2 to 3 weeks spring to autumn.

General Care:
- Keep out of draughts and cold blasts of air.
- Very sensitive to changes in environment.
- Grows best when pot bound.

Troubleshooting:
- Leaf drop; unexpected change in environment, see below.
- Root rot; over watering.

Pests & Diseases:
- Relatively free from pests and diseases.

> **Winter Care:**
> Radermachera are fast growing so will need pruning in late autumn. Lightly trim and reduce watering accordingly. Keep in a warm, well-lit draught free spot.

> **Family:** Bignoniaceae.
> **Genus:** Radermachera.
> **Origin:** South-East Asia.

Radermachera sinica

Rhapis

Common Name: **Bamboo palm, Lady palm**

Rhapis excelsa

Plant Notes: Pronounced 'RAP-is.' As its common name suggests, this slow growing, elegant palm is smaller than most fan palms, making it suitable for a house or apartment. CO_2

Type: Palm.
Colour: Glossy green.
Ideal Spot: Any shady, warm room.
Height: Medium. 60cm/24".
Skill Level: Easy.
Longevity: 5 + years.

Essential Care:
- **Temperature:** Warm/hot. 15–27°C/60–80°F.
- **Watering:** Water thoroughly spring to autumn.
- **Humidity:** Medium. Mist weekly.
- **Light:** Indirect or partial shade.
- **Feeding:** Monthly, spring to autumn.

General Care:
- Never let the plant sit in water.
- Reduce watering and stop feeding in winter.
- Can go outside in summer in a shady spot.
- Avoid draughts and temperature fluctuations.

Troubleshooting:
- Brown tips on leaves; too dry or too warm.

Pests & Diseases:
- Red spider mite.

Trivia:
This elegant palm is an attractive addition to any houseplant collection and is also highly rated by NASA for removing toxins from the air.

Family: Arecaceae.
Genus: Rhapis.
Origin: Southern China.

Rhipsalis

Common Name: Mistletoe cactus, Chain cactus

Plant Notes: Pronounced 'RHIP-sarl-is.' A trailing plant which attaches itself to trees in its natural habitat making it ideal for hanging baskets. Small white flowers are followed by inedible berries that resemble mistletoe.

Type: Forest cactus.
Colour: Mid green.
Ideal Spot: North or west facing aspect.

Trails: up to 90cm/36".
Skill Level: Average.
Longevity: 5 + years.

Essential Care:
- **Temperature:** Warm/hot. 15–27°C/60–80°F.
- **Watering:** Water thoroughly in growing period.
- **Humidity:** Medium. Mist weekly, use pebble tray.
- **Light:** Indirect, filtered light, away from direct sun.
- **Feeding:** Once a month April to September.

General Care:
- Use orchid compost which should be allowed to dry out slightly in between watering.
- Likes fresh air, can go outside in warm summers.
- Don't move plant once buds appear.

Troubleshooting:
- Soft, drooping foliage; too wet or in a draught.

Pests & Diseases:
- Mealy bugs.

Winter Care:
Stop feeding and water only sparingly. Damaged stems can be trimmed off, left to callous over then re-potted in a sand and peat mixture. Winter minimum temperature of 10–15°C/50–55°F.

Family: Cactaceae.
Genus: Rhipsalis.
Origin: Central & South America.

Rhipsalis baccifera

Rhododendron

Common Name: **Indian or Japanese azalea**

Plant Notes: Pronounced 'Row-dow-DEN-dron.' A colourful plant with small, dark green oval leaves bearing single or double flowers, some with a contrasting coloured edge. It can bloom for weeks under the right conditions.

Type: Flowering houseplant.
Colour: Red, cerise, pink, apricot, white.
Ideal Spot: Cool, light windowsill.
Height: Medium. 45cm/18".
Skill Level: Average.
Longevity: 2 + years.

Essential Care:
- **Temperature:** Cool/warm. 10–18°C/50–65°F.
- **Watering:** Keep compost moist, using immersion method.
- **Humidity:** Low. Mist occasionally avoiding wetting flowers.
- **Light:** Bright but shield from direct sun.
- **Feeding:** Every two weeks spring to autumn.

General Care:
- Use ericaceous compost and soft or distilled water.
- Never let the root ball dry out, but don't let plant sit in water.
- Deadhead regularly to encourage more blooms.
- Can go outside in summer and autumn; not frost hardy.
- Keep away from direct heat sources and draughts.

Troubleshooting:
- Shrivelled leaves; underwatering.
- Dry, dropping leaves; too hot or air is too dry.
- Yellowing leaves; too much lime in water.

Pests & Diseases:
- Not overly prone to pests and diseases.

After Flowering:
Place plant in a cool, but bright spot maximum 13°C/55°F. Keep watering and prune back stems by a third to encourage new growth. Move to a slightly warmer spot when buds appear.

Family: Ericaceae.
Genus: Rhododendron.
Origin: East Asia.

Rhododendron simsii

Rosa

Common Name: **Patio rose, Mini rose**

Plant Notes: Pronounced 'Rows-a.' Due to improvements in breeding and production in The Netherlands and Denmark, good quality patio roses are now available all year round in a wide range of colours.

Type: Flowering houseplant.
Colour: All except blue, purple and green.
Ideal Spot: Any sunny room or patio.
Height: Mini/small. 30cm/12".
Skill Level: Easy.
Longevity: 2 + years.

Essential Care:
- **Temperature:** Warm. 10–21°C/50–70°F.
- **Watering:** Keep compost moist, let it dry out slightly between watering.
- **Humidity:** Medium. Avoid wetting flowers. Stand in pebble tray.
- **Light:** A bright, sunny spot, protect from sun scorch.
- **Feeding:** Weekly while in flower.

General Care:
- Needs good air circulation.
- Don't let the root ball dry out.
- Likes fresh air, can go outside in summer.

Troubleshooting:
- Plant becoming leggy; prune back to a bud just above compost level.
- Dry, curled up leaves; underwatering.
- Mould; not enough air circulation.

Pests & Diseases:
- Red spider mite, aphids, blackspot, botrytis.

After Flowering:
Move the plant outside and repot in autumn, pruning the stems by approximately 50%. Reacclimatise in a cool room before bringing it back into the warmth, water regularly.

Family: Rosaceae.
Genus: Rosa.
Origin: Far East.

Rosa

Saintpaulia

Common Name: African violet

Plant Notes: Pronounced 'Saint-PAUL-lee-uh.' A compact plant with richly coloured single or double flowers and hairy, heart-shaped leaves. Often found as part of an indoor planted design.

Type: Flowering houseplant.
Colour: Purple, violet, magenta, pink, white.
Ideal Spot: Warm, bright room.
Height: Mini/small. 20cm/8".
Skill Level: Average.
Longevity: 1–2 years.

Essential Care:
- **Temperature:** Warm/hot. 15–24°C/60–75°F.
- **Watering:** Keep compost moist, always water from below with tepid water.
- **Humidity:** Medium. Use a pebble tray, avoid wetting leaves.
- **Light:** Bright but protect from direct sun.
- **Feeding:** Monthly during spring and summer.

General Care:
- Stand the plant in shallow water for approximately 20 minutes before removing and letting it drain.
- Allow it to dry out slightly in between watering.
- Deadhead regularly.
- Keep out of draughts and sudden changes in temperature.

Troubleshooting:
- Black mould; too damp. Pick out all affected stems and leaves.
- Limp leaves, rotten crown; overwatering.
- No flowers; not enough light or too cold.

Pests & Diseases:
- Whitefly, mealy bugs, cyclamen mite, mildew.

Winter Care:
They need a sunny windowsill in winter, preferably in a kitchen or bathroom as they appreciate the warmth and humidity. Reduce watering slightly always using tepid water.

Family: Gesneriaceae.
Genus: Saintpaulia.
Origin: South Africa.

Saintpaulia ionantha

Sansevieria

Common Name: Snake plant, Mother-in-law's tongue

Plant Notes: Pronounced 'Sans-SEE-var-ri-uh.' Tolerant of most conditions, Sansevieria are almost indestructible. Dramatic, upright leaves have a marbled effect often with striking cream margins.

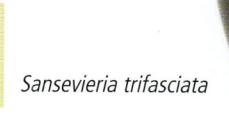

Type: Succulent.
Colour: Dark green, cream variegation.
Ideal Spot: Any bright, warm room.

Height: Medium. 60cm/24".
Skill Level: Easy.
Longevity: 5 + years.

Essential Care:
- **Temperature:** Warm/hot. 15–24°C/60–75°F.
- **Watering:** Don't over soak and let compost dry out slightly in between.
- **Humidity:** Low. Mist occasionally in warm weather.
- **Light:** Bright, or semi-shade but will tolerate some direct sun.
- **Feeding:** Monthly with diluted feed from spring to autumn.

General Care:
- Overwatering can be fatal, never let the plant sit in water.
- Can be top heavy, using a clay pot will off-set this.
- Protect from cold and reduce watering November to February.

Troubleshooting:
- Plant rot at base; over watering or too cold in winter.

Pests & Diseases:
- Relatively free from pests and diseases.

Propagation:
Straightforward, by carefully removing offshoots from the main rhizome. Use a sharp knife and let the cut part of the rhizome seal over before potting it up.

Family: Asparagaceae.
Genus: Sansevieria.
Origin: Africa & Southern Asia.

Sansevieria trifasciata

Sarracenia

Common Name: **Pitcher plant**

Plant Notes: Pronounced 'Sarra-SCENE-nee-uh.' This carnivorous plant entices insects with a rim of nectar around the top of its pitchers. Once they have fallen inside, they are unable to escape and eventually die, the plant then absorbs their nutrients.

Type: Carnivorous.
Colour: Translucent green, red, yellow.
Ideal Spot: Brightly lit windowsill.
Height: Small. 30cm/12".
Skill Level: Average.
Longevity: 3 + years.

Essential Care:
- **Temperature:** Warm/hot. 10–27°C/50–80°F.
- **Watering:** Stand in a saucer of distilled or rainwater spring to autumn.
- **Humidity:** Medium. Mist occasionally with water as above.
- **Light:** Bright, minimum 4 to 5 hours a day, with some direct sun.
- **Feeding:** It will feed itself…don't use plant food.

General Care:
- Can use orchid compost which should be kept moist over winter when the plant is dormant.
- It needs cooler winter temperatures of 4–13°C/40–55°F.
- Prefers to be kept slightly pot bound.
- Don't stand the plant in water over winter.

Troubleshooting:
- Pitchers dying at base; rhizome rot, never wet the crown of the plant.

Pests & Diseases:
- Scale insects, mealy bugs, aphids.

Trivia:
The Venus Fly Trap (*Dionaea muscipula*), which shares the same growing conditions as Sarracenia, is famous for catching insects by snapping its ferocious looking toothed leaves together.

Family: Sarraceniaceae.
Genus: Sarracenia.
Origin: North America.

Sarracenia mitchelliana

Schefflera

Common Name: **Umbrella tree**

Plant Notes: Pronounced 'Chef-LER-uh.' A classic houseplant with attractive palmate green or variegated glossy leaves and elegant upright growth. There are both dwarf and specimen varieties available.

Type: Foliage houseplant.
Colour: Glossy green; cream variegation.
Ideal Spot: Any light, warm room.
Height: Medium/tall. 90cm/36".
Skill Level: Easy.
Longevity: 10 + years.

Essential Care:
- **Temperature:** Warm. 15–24°C/60–75°F.
- **Watering:** Weekly, spring to autumn.
- **Humidity:** Medium. Mist occasionally, use pebble tray.
- **Light:** Bright, avoiding direct sun, will tolerate some shade.
- **Feeding:** Every two weeks spring to autumn.

General Care:
- Allow the compost to dry out slightly in between watering.
- Good drainage is important, it dislikes being too wet.
- Prune any leggy growth to keep the plant in check.
- Can use a moss pole to support it as it grows.

Troubleshooting:
- Foliage turning brown; underwatering.
- Yellow, dropping foliage; compost is too wet.

Pests & Diseases:
- Relatively free from pests and diseases.

Winter Care:
Reduce watering in winter to every 3 to 4 weeks and stop feeding. If keeping the plant in a centrally heated room move it away from direct heat, but keep it out of cold and draughts.

Family: Araliaceae.
Genus: Schefflera.
Origin: Subtropical Asia & Australia.

Schefflera arboricola

Schlumbergera

Common Name: Christmas cactus

Plant Notes: Pronounced 'Shlum-BER-ger-uh.' Brightening up the home in winter, this classic trailing plant has jointed flat stems and vivid flowers. An ideal candidate for a hanging basket.

Type: Forest cactus.
Colour: Mid-green; red, pink, white.
Ideal Spot: Warm, well-lit and out of draughts.
Trails: up to 45cm/18".
Skill Level: Average.
Longevity: 10 + years.

Essential Care:
- **Temperature:** Warm. 13–21°C/55–70°F.
- **Watering:** Keep compost moist with tepid water or rainwater.
- **Humidity:** Medium. Mist foliage, not flowers and use a pebble tray.
- **Light:** Bright, well-lit spot, shaded from direct sun.
- **Feeding:** Monthly, spring to autumn.

General Care:
- Allow the plant to dry out slightly in between watering.
- Don't move the plant once buds have set as this will cause them to drop.
- Can use specialist orchid compost.
- Likes fresh air, can go outside in summer.

Troubleshooting:
- Shrivelling leaves; compost is too dry.
- No flowers; too warm during rest period.

Pests & Diseases:
- Scale insects, mealy bugs.

After Flowering:
Reduce watering, stop feeding and move to a cooler spot, approximately 12–15°C/55–60°F. Resume regular watering and feeding in spring. Reduce watering again slightly in autumn until buds start to show.

Family: Cactaceae.
Genus: Schlumbergera.
Origin: Brazil.

Schlumbergera truncata

Scindapsus

Common Name: **Silver vine, Satin pothos**

Plant Notes: Pronounced 'SKIN-dap-sus.' A vigorous evergreen climbing vine with heart shaped leaves that have a distinctive marbling on their surface. Unfussy, it is a good starter plant.

Type: Foliage climber.
Colour: Deep green, silver/white.
Ideal Spot: Any room in the house.

Height: Tall. 2m/6'.
Skill Level: Easy.
Longevity: 10 + years.

Essential Care:
- **Temperature:** Warm/hot. 15–24°C/60–75°F.
- **Watering:** Keep moist but not waterlogged, spring to autumn.
- **Humidity:** Low. Mist occasionally in warmer weather.
- **Light:** Bright, indirect light, will tolerate some shade.
- **Feeding:** Monthly, spring to autumn.

General Care:
- Allow the plant to dry out slightly in between watering.
- Reduce watering in winter.
- Also suitable for a hanging basket.
- Pinch out growing tips to keep it bushy.

Troubleshooting:
- Leaf drop; compost too damp or not enough light.

Pests & Diseases:
- Relatively free from pests and diseases.

Trivia:
Scindapsus is almost indistinguishable from Epipremnum, or Devil's Ivy. Both plants are highly rated by NASA for their air purification ability.

Family: Araceae.
Genus: Scindapsus.
Origin: South-East Asia.

Scindapsus aureus
Syn. *Epipremnum aureum*

Selaginella

Common Name: Creeping moss, Meadow spike moss

Plant Notes: Pronounced 'Sell-lah-gi-NEL-uh.' Selaginella forms a dense mat of mossy foliage which can be used as ground cover in a mixed planted design or terrarium.

Type: Foliage houseplant.
Colour: Rich green; cream variegation.
Ideal Spot: Bathroom, kitchen or terrarium.
Height: Mini. 15cm/6".
Skill Level: Average.
Longevity: 2 + years.

Essential Care:
- **Temperature:** Warm. 10–24°C/50–75°F.
- **Watering:** Keep compost moist at all times, but not soggy.
- **Humidity:** High. Mist regularly and use a pebble tray.
- **Light:** Semi-shade, out of direct sun.
- **Feeding:** Every 6 to 8 weeks.

General Care:
- Try not to oversoak leaves when misting.
- Pinch out leaf tips to keep the plant bushy and compact.
- Remove damaged or dead stems as soon as they appear.

Troubleshooting:
- Shrivelling leaves; air is too dry or plant is in a draught.
- Brown patches; too wet.

Pests & Diseases:
- Aphids, red spider mite.

Trivia:
Selaginella has a fascinating defence mechanism if it loses its source of moisture, its leaves roll into tight brown balls and the plant becomes dormant. Once watered it will turn green and start to grow again.

Family: Selaginellaceae.
Genus: Selaginella.
Origin: East Coast America.

Selaginella kraussiana variegatus

Sinningia

Common Name: **Gloxinia**

Plant Notes: Pronounced 'see-NIN-jee-uh.' A pretty summer flowering plant with soft hairy leaves and velvety, trumpet shaped single or double flowered blooms which can be as much as 7cm/3" across.

Type: Flowering houseplant.
Colour: White, red, pink, purple, blue.
Ideal Spot: Cool but sunny windowsill.
Height: Small. 30cm/12".
Skill Level: Expert.
Longevity: 2 + years.

Essential Care:
- **Temperature:** Cool/warm. 15–18°C/60–65°F.
- **Watering:** Keep compost moist using tepid water.
- **Humidity:** High. Mist air around plant daily, use pebble tray.
- **Light:** Bright but protect from direct sun.
- **Feeding:** Every two weeks during flowering period.

General Care:
- Flowers spring and summer.
- Try not to wet flowers when misting.
- Never let the plant stand in a draught.
- Direct summer sun will scorch the soft leaves.

Troubleshooting:
- Curled leaves with brown tips; air is too dry.
- Bud drop; dry air or plant is in a draught.
- Plant collapse; overwatering.

Pests & Diseases:
- Susceptible to botrytis.

After Flowering:
Once leaves start yellowing, stop feeding and watering so tuber can dry out. Store dry and frost free over winter. Repot in spring, hollow side up, level with surface of compost. Once leaves show, resume watering and feeding.

Family: Gesneriaceae.
Genus: Sinningia.
Origin: Brazil.

Sinningia

Solanum

Common Name: **Winter cherry, Jerusalem cherry**

Plant Notes: Pronounced 'so-LAN-num.' A popular Christmas plant with small oval green leaves topped by brightly coloured berries in winter which are preceded by pretty white flowers in summer.

Type: Decorative houseplant.
Colour: Orange/red berries, white flowers.
Ideal Spot: Cool with indirect light.
Height: Medium. 60cm/24".
Skill Level: Easy.
Longevity: 2 + years.

Essential Care:
- **Temperature:** Cool/warm. 10–15°C/50–60°F.
- **Watering:** Keep compost moist, spring to winter.
- **Humidity:** Low. Mist occasionally if in a centrally heated room.
- **Light:** Bright, indirect light.
- **Feeding:** Monthly from spring until fruits appear.

General Care:
- The non-edible berries are initially green before they turn orange.
- Allow compost to dry out slightly in between watering.
- Can go outside in a cool shady spot in summer.

Troubleshooting:
- Leaf drop; waterlogged compost.
- Berry drop; too shady or not enough humidity.

Pests & Diseases:
- Whitefly, red spider mite, aphids, botrytis.

Solanum pseudocapsicum

After Fruiting:
In early spring, prune stems by approximately half. Reduce watering and stop feeding for 6 to 8 weeks. Place outside in a sunny spot in summer, bring back inside in autumn.

Family: Solanaceae.
Genus: Solanaceae.
Origin: Peru & Ecuador.

Soleirolia

Common Name: Mind your own business, Baby's tears

Plant Notes: Pronounced 'so-ley-ROH-lee-uh.' A mossy mound of tiny leaves which makes excellent background cover in mixed planted designs where it will act as a foil to more colourful specimens.

Type: Foliage houseplant.
Colour: Lime, sage, dark green.
Ideal Spot: Terrarium or light, humid room.
Spread: 10 x 90cm/4 x 36".
Skill Level: Easy.
Longevity: 5 + years.

Essential Care:
- **Temperature:** Cool/hot. 7–24°C/45–75°F.
- **Watering:** Keep compost moist at all times but not waterlogged.
- **Humidity:** Medium. Mist weekly in hot weather.
- **Light:** Bright indirect light.
- **Feeding:** Monthly, spring and summer.

General Care:
- Never let the compost dry out but reduce watering slightly in winter.
- Can be invasive if not checked, trim to keep in shape.
- Pinch out growing shoots to keep it bushy.

Troubleshooting:
- Leaves turning brown; underwatering.

Pests & Diseases:
- Relatively free from pests and diseases.

> **Propagation:**
> To propagate Soleirolia, divide the plant by pulling it apart and gently pushing a clump onto the surface of a pot of moist compost, use a hairpin to secure it.

Family: Urticaceae.
Genus: Soleirolia.
Origin: Western Mediterranean.

Soleirolia soleirolii

Solenostemon

Common Name: Coleus, Flame nettle

Plant Notes: Pronounced 'SOL-len-e-o-stem-on. Familiar in summer bedding schemes and an attractive addition to indoor plant collections. Intensely coloured leaves and a bushy habit make this perennial a standout plant.

Type: Foliage houseplant.
Colour: Red, pink, orange, yellow, green, burgundy.
Ideal Spot: Sunny room or outside patio.
Height: Small. 30cm/12".
Skill Level: Easy.
Longevity: 6–12 months.

Essential Care:
- **Temperature:** Warm/hot. 13–21°C/55–70°F.
- **Watering:** Water well, keeping compost moist but not soggy.
- **Humidity:** Low. Mist occasionally, especially if indoors.
- **Light:** Bright, indirect light.
- **Feeding:** Once a month spring to autumn.

General Care:
- At its peak April to September.
- Pinch out growing tips for a bushier plant.
- Can be recycled at the end of summer.
- If keeping over winter however, prune back in spring.

Troubleshooting:
- Leaf drop; either too hot or too dry.

Pests & Diseases:
- Red spider mite.

Trivia:
Coleus has recently been reclassified into the closely related genus Solenostemon. In turn, some Solenostemon were reclassified into the genus Plectranthus.

Family: Lamiaceae.
Genus: Solenostemon.
Origin: Tropical Africa & Asia.

Solenostemon spp.
Syn. *Coleus*

Spathiphyllum

Common Name: **Peace lily**

Plant Notes: Pronounced 'Spath-ee-PHIL-um.' An elegant plant with slim, glossy leaves. Its long-lasting 'flower' is a spadix surrounded by a tear-shaped spathe which will gradually turn green with age.

Type: Flowering houseplant.
Colour: Dark green; white.
Ideal Spot: Warm, semi-shaded room.

Height: Medium. 60cm/24".
Skill Level: Easy.
Longevity: 10 + years.

Essential Care:
- **Temperature:** Warm/hot. 13–24°C/55–75°F.
- **Watering:** Keep compost moist, but not waterlogged.
- **Humidity:** Medium. Mist leaves regularly and use pebble tray.
- **Light:** Bright to semi-shade, out of direct sun.
- **Feeding:** Every two weeks spring to autumn.

General Care:
- Flowers spring and summer.
- Protect from cold and draughts.
- Clean leaves occasionally with a damp cloth.

Troubleshooting:
- Failure to flower; not enough feed or too dark.
- Wilting leaves; too dry.
- Yellowing leaves; too light, sunlight will scorch leaves.

Pests & Diseases:
- Red spider mite, aphids, mealy bugs.

> **After Flowering:**
> Carefully remove flower stems after blooming. Reduce watering during autumn and winter and stop feeding. Resume watering and feeding as normal in early spring.

Family: Araceae.
Genus: Spathiphyllum.
Origin: Tropical Americas & South-East Asia.

Spathiphyllum wallisii

Stephanotis

Common Name: **Madagascar jasmine**

Plant Notes: Pronounced 'STEF-ann-oh-tis.' Highly scented waxy flowers are borne in clusters above glossy green leaves. A vigorous climber which can be trained around a hoop or encouraged to grow on trellis.

Type: Flowering climber.
Colour: Glossy green; creamy white.
Ideal Spot: Warm, sunny windowsill.
Height: Medium/tall. 60cm–3m/24"–10'.
Skill Level: Expert.
Longevity: 5 + years.

Essential Care:
- **Temperature:** Warm/hot. 15–24°C/60–75°F.
- **Watering:** Keep compost moist using tepid water.
- **Humidity:** High. Mist in the morning, use pebble tray.
- **Light:** Bright spot with indirect sunlight.
- **Feeding:** Every two weeks spring to autumn.

General Care:
- Summer flowering; may rebloom in autumn.
- Allow the plant to dry out slightly between watering.
- Avoid sudden changes in temperature.
- Try not to move plant once flower buds have set.

Troubleshooting:
- Leaf curl or plant collapse; compost too wet.
- Failure to flower; air too dry or cold, or insufficient winter rest.
- Bud drop; any sudden changes in care or environment.

Pests & Diseases:
- Mealy bugs, scale insects.

Winter Care:
Stephanotis require cooler winters, around 13°C/55°F is ideal, but no lower than 10°C/50°F. Stop feeding and reduce watering. Trim back in spring and refresh the top layer of compost.

Family: Apocynaceae.
Genus: Stephanotis.
Origin: Madagascar.

Stephanotis floribunda

Streptocarpus

Common Name: **Cape primrose**

Plant Notes: Pronounced 'STREP-toe-car-pus.' A free-flowering plant with showy, trumpet shaped blooms often bi-coloured. The foliage forms an attractive rosette of lance shaped leaves.
Type: Flowering houseplant.
Colour: White, blue, purple, red, pink.
Ideal Spot: Bright, but out of direct sun.
Height: Small. 30cm/12".
Skill Level: Easy.
Longevity: 5 + years.

Essential Care:
- **Temperature:** Warm. 13–24°C/55–75°F.
- **Watering:** Allow compost to dry out slightly between watering.
- **Humidity:** Medium. Mist leaves, not flowers, use pebble tray.
- **Light:** Bright; shade from direct sun which will scorch leaves.
- **Feeding:** In summer with a high potash feed if possible.

General Care:
- Summer flowering, deadhead regularly spring to autumn.
- Keep out of draughts and cold air.
- Keeping them slightly pot bound will produce more flowers.

Troubleshooting:
- Wilting plant; overwatering.
- Shrivelled or drooping leaves; air is too dry.

Pests & Diseases:
- Relatively free from pests and diseases.

After Flowering:
Stop feeding and reduce watering, keeping it slightly on the dry side. Place in a cool, bright spot until March when it can be re-potted and normal watering and feeding resumed.

Family: Gesneriaceae.
Genus: Streptocarpus.
Origin: Southern Africa.

Streptocarpus hybrid

Syngonium

Common Name: **Goosefoot plant**

Plant Notes:	Pronounced 'Sin-GO-nee-um.' A popular variegated plant which will need support as it grows. The distinctive arrow shaped leaves change to a five lobed form as they mature.
Type:	Foliage houseplant.
Colour:	Bright green, cream variegation.
Ideal Spot:	Kitchen or bathroom.

Height: Medium. 60cm/24".
Skill Level: Average.
Longevity: 5 + years.

Essential Care:
- **Temperature:** Warm/hot. 15–27°C/60–80°F.
- **Watering:** Keep compost moist, but not waterlogged.
- **Humidity:** Medium. Mist regularly, use pebble tray.
- **Light:** Well-lit spot, but out of direct sun.
- **Feeding:** Every two weeks, spring to autumn.

General Care:
- Allow the plant to dry out slightly between watering.
- Will tolerate light shade.
- All parts are poisonous, wash hands after handling.

Troubleshooting:
- Soft leaves brown at edges; overwatering.
- Leaves losing variegation; too dark.

Pests & Diseases:
- Mealy bugs, red spider mite.

Winter Care:
Reduce watering, just keeping compost on the damp side and stop feeding. Prune in spring to keep it bushy and top dress with fresh compost. Winter minimum temperature 15°/60°F.

Family: Araceae.
Genus: Syngonium.
Origin: South & Central America.

Syngonium podophyllum

Tolmiea

Common Name: **Pickaback plant**

Plant Notes: Pronounced 'TOL-mee-uh.' Soft, downy maple-like foliage belie this plants hard to keep reputation. Its common name comes from the little plantlets which form on the back of mature leaves.

Type: Foliage houseplant.
Colour: Mottled dark to lime green foliage.
Ideal Spot: Cool, well-ventilated in semi-shade.
Height: Small. 30cm/12".
Skill Level: Expert.
Longevity: 1–2 years.

Essential Care:
- **Temperature:** Cool. 7–15°C/45–60°F.
- **Watering:** Keep compost moist throughout spring and summer.
- **Humidity:** High. Mist frequently, use pebble tray.
- **Light:** Semi-shade, out of direct sun.
- **Feeding:** Every two weeks spring to autumn.

General Care:
- Protect from draughts and direct heat sources.
- Give it plenty of space to allow plantlets to develop.
- Trim back any winter damaged foliage in spring.

Troubleshooting:
- Wilting leaves; air is too dry or too warm.
- Plant collapse; too wet, reduce watering in winter.

Pests & Diseases:
- Red spider mite, aphids, mealy bugs.

Tolmiea menziesii

Propagation:
Remove and pot up plantlets from mid to late summer by pushing them gently into moist compost. Can use a wire pin or similar to secure them.

Family: Saxifragaceae.
Genus: Tolmiea.
Origin: West coast of North America.

Tradescantia

Common Name: Silver-inch plant

Plant Notes: Pronounced 'TRAD-es-scan-tee-uh.' An energetic trailing plant, fast growing with attractive striped variegation and purple underside to its leaves. A good plant for the non-green fingered!

Type: Foliage houseplant.
Colour: Green, cream, pale pink, silver.
Ideal Spot: Hanging basket in draught free spot.
Trails: 15–60cm/6-24".
Skill Level: Easy.
Longevity: 5 + years.

Essential Care:
- **Temperature:** Warm/hot. 13–24°C/55–75°F.
- **Watering:** Keep compost moist but not waterlogged.
- **Humidity:** Low. Mist occasionally if in a centrally heated room.
- **Light:** Bright with some indirect sunshine.
- **Feeding:** Weekly, spring to summer.

General Care:
- Allow the plant to dry out slightly between watering.
- Display away from draughts and direct heat sources.
- Pinch out growing tips to encourage bushy growth.

Troubleshooting:
- Spindly growth; too dark or not enough water.
- Loss of variegation; too dark.
- Brown leaf tips; air is too dry.

Pests & Diseases:
- Red spider mite, greenfly.

Propagation:
Very easily, by taking young stem cuttings in spring and pushing them into moist compost. A number of cuttings can be planted into the same pot; they should root between 6 to 8 weeks.

Family: Commelinaceae.
Genus: Tradescantia.
Origin: North & Central America.

Tradescantia spp.

Vanda

Common Name: **Vanda**

Plant Notes:	Pronounced 'VAN-duh.' A stunning orchid with large, impressive five petaled flowers. Orchid compost is not needed, instead, suspend plants in a wire basket where both leaves and roots are exposed and can be admired.
Type:	Orchid.
Colour:	Blue, purple, orange, red, yellow.
Ideal Spot:	Greenhouse, conservatory.
Height:	Medium/tall. 90cm/36".
Skill Level:	Expert.
Longevity:	5 + years.

Essential Care:
- **Temperature:** Hot. 15–32°C/60–90°F.
- **Watering:** Daily by immersion using tepid water or rainwater.
- **Humidity:** High. Mist roots and leaves daily.
- **Light:** Bright sunshine but shield from direct sun through glass.
- **Feeding:** Mist weekly with orchid fertiliser while in flower.

General Care:
- Can also be grown in a glass vase.
- Will flower two or three times a year.
- A lower night temperature, 15–21°C/60–70°F will encourage buds to form.
- Reduce watering and misting in winter.

Troubleshooting:
- Leaves becoming dark green; not enough light.

Pests & Diseases:
- Relatively free from pests and diseases.

> **Trivia:**
> Vandas are epiphytic and grow high on the sides of trees in forests, getting water and nutrients from the rain and air around them. This explains their love of warmth and humidity.

Family: Orchidaceae.
Genus: Vanda.
Origin: Asia, India & Australasia.

Vanda

Vriesea

Common Name: **Flaming sword**

Plant Notes: Pronounced 'Ver-RE-see-uh.' Banded, arching leaves combined with a brightly coloured, long-lasting central flowering bract make this a stand-out Bromeliad. Good for beginners.

Type: Bromeliad.
Colour: Green; red bract with yellow flowers.
Ideal Spot: Warm room with indirect light.
Height: Small/medium. 60cm/24".
Skill Level: Easy.
Longevity: Flowers 3–6 months.

Essential Care:
- **Temperature:** Warm/hot. 18–26°C/64–79°F.
- **Watering:** With distilled or rainwater into the central 'vase' of the plant.
- **Humidity:** Medium. Mist every 3 to 4 days.
- **Light:** Bright, indirect light, shade from direct sun.
- **Feeding:** Monthly, spring to autumn.

General Care:
- Water compost, allowing it to dry out slightly in between.
- Avoid handling the bract and flowers.
- Keep compost moist in summer, water less in winter.

Troubleshooting:
- Brown tips to leaves; air is too dry.
- Blotches on leaves; a reaction to hard water.

Pests & Diseases:
- Relatively free from pests and diseases.

After Flowering:
The mother plant will die off, but new plantlets will form that can be re-potted. Reduce watering and stop feeding over winter, minimum winter temperature 13°C/55°F. See page 133.

Family: Bromeliaceae.
Genus: Vriesea.
Origin: Central & South America.

Vriesea spp.

Wallisia

Common Name: **Pink quill**

Plant Notes: Pronounced 'Wall-IS-see-uh.' This baby Bromeliad has a solid, flat, oval flower head made up of pink bracts which produce tiny flowers down each side. It is neat, compact and easy to care for.

Type: Bromeliad.
Colour: Grey/green; violet-blue, pink.
Ideal Spot: Bathroom or kitchen.
Height: Small. 30cm/12".
Skill Level: Easy.
Longevity: 1–2 years.

Essential Care:
- **Temperature:** Warm/hot. 15–24°C/60–75°F.
- **Watering:** Keep compost moist using tepid or rainwater.
- **Humidity:** High. Mist frequently, use pebble tray.
- **Light:** Bright, indirect shade from direct sun.
- **Feeding:** Monthly, use diluted feed when misting.

Wallisia Ionantha

General Care:
- Water by immersion, allowing plant to drain thoroughly afterwards.
- When misting, avoid wetting the bract and flowers.
- Once it has flowered the parent plant will die.
- New plantlets will form to replace the original plant.

Troubleshooting:
- No flowers; not enough light.
- Brown tips on leaves; air or compost too dry.

Pests & Diseases:
- Relatively free from pests and diseases.

Air Plants:
Known as Grey Tillandsias, air plants don't require compost, they absorb nutrients and water through their foliage. Display them on decorative pieces of wood, misting monthly.

Family: Bromeliaceae.
Genus: Wallisia.
Origin: South Africa.

Wallisia cyanea
Syn. *Tillandsia cyanea*

Yucca

Common Name: **Yucca, Spineless Yucca**

Plant Notes: Pronounced 'YUCK-uh.' An impressive sculptural plant with sword-like leaves that grow in upright rosettes from a solid trunk. An excellent specimen plant for large rooms and offices.

Type: Foliage houseplant.
Colour: Dark green.
Ideal Spot: Large sunny room.
Height: Tall. 90cm/36".
Skill Level: Easy.
Longevity: 10 + years.

Essential Care:
- **Temperature:** Warm/hot. 10–27°C/50–80°F.
- **Watering:** Let the compost dry out slightly between watering.
- **Humidity:** Low. Misting not necessary.
- **Light:** Bright and sunny, will tolerate some direct sun.
- **Feeding:** Once a month spring to autumn.

General Care:
- Never let the plant stand in water.
- Needs a deep container with good drainage.
- Can go outside in summer in a sheltered, sunny spot.
- Use a damp cloth to clean leaves.

Troubleshooting:
- Yellowing leaves; not enough light.
- Brown leaves; compost is too wet.

Pests & Diseases:
- Scale insects.

Winter Care:
Yuccas need a cool, frost free spot over winter, minimum 7°C/45°F. Reduce watering to once a month and stop feeding. Re-pot every 2 to 3 years.

Family: Asparagaceae.
Genus: Yucca.
Origin: Mexico & Guatemala.

Yucca elephantipes

Zamioculcas

Common Name: **Fern arum, ZZ plant**

Plant Notes: Pronounced 'Zam-ee-oh-KUL-kass.' A relatively new introduction into the houseplant market, these unusual plants have upright rubbery leaves divided into leaflets which have a feathery appearance.

Type: Foliage houseplant.
Colour: Dark green.
Ideal Spot: Any room in the house.

Height: Tall. 90cm/36".
Skill Level: Easy.
Longevity: 5 + years.

Essential Care:
- **Temperature:** Warm/hot. 15–24°C/60–75°F.
- **Watering:** Allow compost to dry out slightly between watering.
- **Humidity:** Low. Mist occasionally.
- **Light:** Indirect bright light, will tolerate some shade.
- **Feeding:** Once a month spring to autumn.

General Care:
- Keep out of draughts and cold.
- Reduce watering to once a month autumn and winter.
- Can prune back lightly in spring.

Troubleshooting:
- Wilting, soft foliage; compost is too wet.
- Brown patches on leaves; sun scorch.

Pests & Diseases:
- Relatively free from pests and diseases.

> **Trivia:**
> It was in 1999 that Florida growers first started production of this easy to care for plant. In 2002 it was named as their Indoor Houseplant of the Year.

Family: Araceae.
Genus: Zamioculcas.
Origin: Eastern Africa.

Zamioculcas zamiifolia

Zantedeschia

Common Name: Calla lily

Plant Notes: Pronounced 'ZANT-ee-desh-e-uh.' A stately and impressive plant with broad, arrow shaped leaves and single trumpet shaped blooms in strong, bold colours. Leaves can be plain or spotted.

Type: Flowering houseplant.
Colour: White, yellow, pink, red, maroon.
Ideal Spot: Humid with light shade.
Height: Medium. 60cm/24".
Skill Level: Average.
Longevity: 2–3 years.

Essential Care:
- **Temperature:** Warm. 10–21°C/50–70°F.
- **Watering:** Keep compost moist spring and summer.
- **Humidity:** High. Mist every 2 to 3 days, use pebble tray.
- **Light:** Indirect sun to light shade.
- **Feeding:** Every two weeks while in flower.

General Care:
- Flowers spring and summer.
- Grows from a rhizome which can be divided in spring.
- Will not tolerate drying out.
- Likes fresh air, can go outside in summer.

Troubleshooting:
- Soft, wilting leaves; compost is too dry.

Pests & Diseases:
- Aphids and red spider mite.

Winter Care:
When the leaves die down in autumn, repot and overwinter in a cool, frost free place, minimum temperature 10°C/50°F. Reduce watering to a minimum. Resume watering and feeding in early spring.

Family: Araceae.
Genus: Zantedeschia.
Origin: South Africa.

Zantedeschia spp.

Bromeliads & Cacti

Bromeliads. Showy, dramatic and easy to look after.

Natural flowering season: Summer.

Native to: Tropical Americas where they live on trees, rocks or the forest floor. They have shallow root systems so should be kept in shallow pots and not overwatered.

Temperature Range: Warm/hot. 15–27°C/55–80°F.

Watering: With rainwater or distilled water in the central 'vase' of the plant. Also keep the compost moist but not soggy.

Humidity: Medium. Prefers a humid atmosphere.

Light: Indirect.

Feeding: They absorb food through their leaves, use liquid fertiliser in a spray bottle.

Compost: Airy and free draining; can use cactus compost.

Repotting: In spring, using a shallow pot.

Propagation: The mother plant will produce offsets or 'pups' that can be removed once they are about one-third the size of the main plant. Take the plant out of its pot and cut off the pup with a sharp knife. If you have rooting powder dab some on the base. Carefully insert the pup into cactus compost, just below the surface, keep in a warm place and don't overwater.

Desert Cacti. Fascinating and long-lasting.

Natural flowering season: Summer.

Native to: Desert regions of the Americas where days are hot and sunny, but nights are cold, which means that a change in temperature between day and night is beneficial to them.

Temperature Range: Cool to hot. 10–27°C/50–80°F.

Watering: Treat as a normal houseplant in spring and summer, watering when compost starts to dry out. Water very sparingly in winter, just enough to see them through.

Humidity: Low. Fresh air is more important.

Light: Sunny, bright spot.

Feeding: Monthly spring to summer, not required in winter.

Compost: Specialist cactus compost is available.

Repotting: In the spring and only if essential.

Propagation: By offsets (see above) or cuttings taken in the spring, the base of the cutting must be allowed to callous over before being potted up, use cactus compost and water only when top of compost is dry.

Flowering: Cacti will normally flower when mature, being slightly pot bound will encourage them.

Ferns & Orchids

Ferns. Attractive and popular but will not tolerate neglect.

Native to: Found worldwide in sheltered environments with high humidity.

Temperature Range: Warm. 10–24°C/50–75°F. Keep away from direct heat sources and draughts.

Watering: Keep compost moist at all times, but never soggy, reduce watering in winter.

Humidity: High. Mist foliage regularly but don't soak leaves. Stand in pebble tray.

Light: Indirect, but not too shady. A east or north facing windowsill is ideal.

Feeding: Feed when watering in spring and summer, not required in winter.

Compost: Good quality multipurpose compost.

Repotting: In spring if roots are showing through pot, leave crown of plant exposed.

Propagation: Ferns reproduce by spores; they do not flower or have seeds. Can repot by division in spring if new shoots appear around base of plant. Water the plant first letting it soak through, then remove from pot and carefully tease out the new shoot leaving as much root on as possible. Repot into fresh compost and keep in a warm spot.

Orchids. Exotic, but easier to care for than you think.

Natural flowering season: Every eight to twelve months.

Native to: Found worldwide in hugely diverse environments. Orchids popular as houseplants, however, tend to come from tropical regions where they grow on trees, rocks and the forest floor.

Temperature Range: Warm/hot 15–27°C/60–80°F. Avoid cold draughts. Prefer cooler nights.

Watering: Keep compost moist and use soft, tepid water. Reduce watering in winter

Humidity: High. Stand in pebble tray, misting leaves and roots in the morning.

Light: Bright, indirect, but lots of it. Also needs good ventilation.

Feeding: During the summer months, with specialised orchid feed.

Compost: Use specialist orchid compost.

Repotting: It is natural for the roots to grow outside of the pot, only repot if absolutely necessary, after 2 to 3 years.

Propagation: By division, or potting up offsets.

After Flowering: Stems that have gone brown, cut back to base. Stems that are still green, cut back to the second or third node to encourage re-flowering. Keep the plant in a brightly lit spot and continue to water and feed as normal. Cooler temperatures at night will also encourage re-flowering.

Palms & Succulents

Palms. Impressive and reliable.

Native to: Tropical and sub-tropical climates.

Temperature Range: Warm. 13–24°C/55–75°F. Slightly cooler in winter. Sensitive to sudden changes in the environment.

Watering: Palms need good drainage; the roots should never be waterlogged. Water well in spring and summer, less in winter.

Humidity: Mist foliage when displayed in centrally heated rooms. If leaves need cleaning, use water and a damp cloth, don't use leafshine.

Light: Partial shade is ideal, but not too dark.

Feeding: Feed when watering in spring and summer, not required in winter.

Compost: Good quality multipurpose compost with good drainage.

Repotting: Palms dislike being disturbed, so repot only if plant is completely pot bound..

Propagation: For the expert, as they can only be propagated from seed.

Keeping them in check: Be aware that the growing point of the leaf is at its tip, so if that is cut back, it will not regrow.

Succulents. Popular compact plants, easy to look after.

Native to: Desert habitats, where their tightly packed rosette shape allows the plant to conserve valuable water.

Temperature Range: Cool to hot. 5–30°C/41–86°F. Generally, keep warm in summer, cool in winter, they appreciate a difference in temperature between day and night.

Watering: In spring and summer water whenever compost starts to dry out. Keep almost dry in winter – overwatering is their biggest killer.

Humidity: Misting not necessary, but they do like a blast of fresh air every now and then.

Light: Bright, south facing windowsill, but shade from direct sun through glass, can go outside in the summer.

Feeding: During the summer months, not necessary in winter.

Compost: Free draining; cactus compost is ideal.

Repotting: Only if necessary and keep to a shallow container.

Propagation: Straightforward by stem cuttings or naturally produced offsets. Allow base of cut or offset to callous over before potting up. Water sparingly.

Caring for Mixed Planted Designs

Planted Containers and Baskets

If you are presented with a collection of green and flowering houseplants which have been planted directly into a container then enjoy it while it's at its best, but don't be afraid to take it apart once it starts to outgrow its space. Left too long, the roots of the plants will entwine and make separation difficult. The plants can then be potted up or planted out individually.

Care of your planted container:

- The container will have no drainage, so water with care avoiding waterlogging compost. .
- Feeding is not necessary for a temporary display.
- Spray occasionally, avoid wetting any flowering plants.
- Display in a bright, warm spot away from direct sun and heat sources.

Indoor Bulbs

A popular Christmas gift, a pot of indoor flowering bulbs will instantly lift the spirits. If the container has no drainage water sparingly and with care. Display where you can enjoy their colourful, but short-lived flowering period.

After Flowering:

- Cut off dead flowers but leave stalks and leaves.
- Water as above and add plant food every two weeks.
- Once all foliage has withered, remove bulbs and allow to dry out.
- Store bulbs in a cool, dry place and replant in the garden in the autumn.

Terrariums and Bottle gardens

Terrariums or bottle gardens are glass containers that provide a microclimate for the plants within. They are ideal for plants that love warm, humid conditions such as ferns, Fittonias and Peperomias. Terrariums can have a compost and moss base, suitable for green plants, or a mix of sand and gravel for succulents and cacti.

Care Instructions:

- The glass container will trap moisture, so water cautiously, letting the growing medium almost dry out first.
- Display in a bright spot but away from direct sunlight which the glass will magnify the intensity of, potentially scorching the plants within.
- Be prepared to replace old plants with new as they grow and mature.

Composts & Re-potting

Compost – What type?

Houseplant Compost
Both houseplant and multipurpose compost are readily available from garden centres and are suitable for the majority of flowering and foliage houseplants. These composts include fertilizer, so newly potted up plants won't need feeding for the first six to eight weeks.

Orchid and Cactus Compost
Formulated to meet these plants specific growing needs, orchid compost is light and contains bark which provides drainage and air circulation. Cactus compost has a high percentage of sand and grit and is also suitable for succulents.

Ericaceous Compost
Developed for plants that are acid loving and lime hating, such as Rhododendron, heather, Camellia and blue Hydrangea (alkaline soil will turn Hydrangeas pink).

Bulb Fibre
Bulbs will rot easily in heavy, wet compost. Bulb fibre is a normally a mixture of peat, plus perlite, which keeps it light, and charcoal which stops the mix from becoming stagnant.

Seed and Cutting Compost
If you have cuttings to propagate, use this specialist compost which is free draining and fine textured.

Re-potting

All plants will eventually outgrow their pot, usually after one or two years. When they do it is time to repot them into something bigger. The easiest way to check if your plant needs repotting is to see if its roots are growing out of the drainage holes at the base or if the plant is wilting and losing colour.

The new pot should only be one size bigger than the old so that the roots don't have too much of a shock. First, water your plant allowing the water to seep through. Add a layer of fresh compost to the bottom of the pot then carefully remove the plant, cutting the old pot off with scissors if necessary. Place the plant into its new pot and fill around the sides with more compost using a spoon or small trowel.

Water and mist the plant, then let it stand undisturbed for a week or two while it gets used to its new home.

Specimen Plants
Large, heavy plants can be difficult to repot, instead top dress the pot in spring. Do this by carefully removing the top 3cm/1" of compost and replace with fresh houseplant or multipurpose compost.

Pests & Diseases

Even with the best intentions, houseplants can fall prey to insect attack or disease. The best way to prevent this is by checking them regularly for the first signs of problems and secondly making sure that their care requirements are correct. Although there are a number of chemical solutions to be found to treat any infestation, a holistic approach is always the best place to start, both for the plant and for the environment.

Pests

Aphids (greenfly and blackfly)

Tiny black or green sap sucking insects which are found in clusters on shoot tips, flower buds and under leaves. They secrete a sticky honeydew. Flowering plants are particularly susceptible.

Treat by wiping off with a cloth soaked in a soap solution (washing up liquid is fine). Gloves are recommended!

Infestation of greenfly

Mealy Bugs

Tiny insects covered in a white fluff which hides them and their eggs. Find them under foliage and in between leaves and stems. They cause leaves to turn yellow, wilt and fall.

Treat with a soapy cloth or methylated spirit on the end of a cotton bud or Q-tip. If the infestation is very bad the plant should be disposed of.

Mealy bugs

Red Spider Mite

Minute sap sucking insects that can infest the underside of leaves, leaving tell-tale webs between leaves and stems. Very common when air is too dry or hot, leaves have a mottled appearance and will drop prematurely. Plants in greenhouses, porches and conservatories are particularly vulnerable.

Treat by wiping with a soap solution and by keeping humidity high and plants at the correct temperature. Heavily infested plants should be thrown away.

Red spider mite

Scale Insects

They look like small brown discs and they attach themselves to the underside of leaves where they suck the sap. If leaves turn yellow and sticky, the plant needs to be discarded.

Treat with a soapy solution or with methylated spirits applied carefully with a cotton bud or Q-tip.

Scale insects

Pests & Diseases

Thrips

Minute black winged flies which leave tiny black spots and a slivery discolouration on leaves. Will distort flowers and stunt growth.

Treat with a glue trap which you can make by coating a small piece of card or plastic with glue which can then be either hung near the plant or pushed temporarily into the compost using a wooden pick.

Close up of a thrip

Whitefly

Tiny but easy to spot as they rise up in clouds when disturbed. They also secrete honeydew so look for a sticky residue. Flowering plants are more prone to infestations.

Treat with a glue trap or a soapy solution, if possible, place the plant outside which can also clear them up. Isolate the plant as they spread easily.

Whitefly

Diseases

The best way to avoid your plants becoming vulnerable is to look after their basic requirements, don't over or underwater or let the plant become damp all of which are scenarios that invite disease.

Black Spot

Leaves will have small black spots which will cause them to drop. Often seen on patio roses.

Remove all affected leaves both on the plant and those that have fallen. Reduce watering, stop misting and improve air circulation.

Botrytis

A fluffy grey mould which often affects soft-tissue plants such as Saintpaulia. Caused by damp and poor ventilation.

Cut away and dispose of affected areas, reduce watering and spraying and increase air circulation.

Root Rot

Plant collapse caused by waterlogged compost, never let a plant stand in water. Plant will need to be disposed of.

Powdery Mildew

A white deposit on leaves, usually caused by a lack of water and poor ventilation.

Remove and dispose of all affected parts. Plant may need to be discarded if it is widespread.

A leaf affected with powdery mildew

Glossary

Botanical and floristry terms

Annual	A plant that completes its entire life cycle in one year.
Bract	A modified leaf, often brightly coloured, spiky or petal-like.
Bulb/Corm	An underground storage bud with fleshy, scaly leaves.
Caging	Enclosing all or part of a design in a three-dimensional manner .
Conditioning	Preparing plant material in advance before using in floral designs.
Cyclamen mite	A tiny mite which nests in damp parts of the plant. Infestation causes misshapen flowers and deformed leaves.
Deadhead	Removing spent flower blooms to prolong flowering.
Decorative houseplant	One which is grown for its fruits or berries and discarded after use.
Dish garden	A miniature garden of small plants within a low bowl or dish.
Distilled water	Purified water, made by boiling into a vapour then condensing back into water.
Dormant	Suspension of active growth, often, but not exclusively over the winter months.
Epiphytic	A plant which depends on another for support, but not nutrients.
Ethylene gas	A colourless, odourless gas produced by plants, fruits and vegetables as they ripen.
Evergreen	A plant which keeps its foliage throughout the year.
Family	A closely related group of flowers and plants sharing common characteristics.
Forest cactus	Cacti found in rainforests that prefer shadier spots and high levels of humidity.
Frost hardy	Able to withstand temperatures down to -5°C/23°F.
Hybrid	Naturally or artificially produced offspring of genetically different parents.
Genus	A subdivision of flowers or plants within a larger family that closely resemble each other.
Immersion	A method of watering where the entire pot is submerged in water until thoroughly soaked. It is then left to drain before being placed back in its pot cover.
Houseplant	An ornamental/decorative plant, flowering and/or green which is grown indoors.
Humidity	Maintaining a level of moisture or water vapour in the air.
Latex	A milky, sometimes sticky sap exuded by certain plants.
Leafshine	A commercial spray designed to give an artificial gloss to leaves.
Moss pole	A wire cylinder filled with sphagnum moss designed to support tall plants.

Glossary

Botanical and floristry terms

Offsets	Young plantlets which grow on mature plants which can be removed and propagated.
Pebble dish/tray	A shallow dish or tray of small pebbles or gravel filled with water. Plants are stood on top to benefit from the humidity created from the rising, evaporating water.
Perennial	A plant that has a life cycle of three or more seasons.
Photosynthesis	The method by which a plant turns carbon dioxide into oxygen.
Pinnate	A leaf divided into two or more leaflets.
Plantlet	A young plant that develops on a mature plant.
Pollination	Transfer by insect, bird, wind, water or hand of pollen from one flower to another.
Pot-bound	A plant whose root system has filled, or nearly filled its pot, some plants prefer to be kept slightly pot-bound depending on their natural habitat.
Prune	To remove twigs or branches to maintain the health, shape or bushiness of the plant or to encourage it to fruit or flower.
Rhizome	Horizontal, fleshy stem which grows underground.
Shrub	A plant with a woody stem and which is usually branched from the base upwards.
Soft water	Surface water which contains low concentrates of calcium and magnesium.
Specimen plant	A tall plant which is grown for its impressive size and appearance.
Stigma	The part of the flower which receives pollen for fertilization.
Stolons	Arching or trailing stems which produce new shoots and roots at their tips.
Synonym/Syn.	A plant name not officially accepted.
Top dress	Removing the old top layer of compost to replace with fresh.
Tuber	An underground stem with ability to store water.
Variegation	Leaves containing two or more colours.
Veiling	Adding delicate materials over more solid forms.
Winding	Using flexible material to wind round other forms for decoration.

Index

Common names and synonyms

African daisy	64	Chinese fan palm	79	Fiddleleaf fig	59
African violet	110	Chinese maple	8	Flame nettle	120
Agave	12	Chinese wool flower	30	Flaming Katy	77
Airplane plant	34	Christmas cactus	114	Flaming sword	128
Aloe	15	Christmas pepper	29	Flamingo flower	17
Aluminium plant	102	Christmas star	55	Florist's cyclamen	48
Amaryllis	70	Cineraria	98	Florist's slipperwort	27
American century plant	12	Cockscomb	30	Flowering maple	8
Arabian violet	56	Coconut palm	39	Foxtail fern	20
Azalea	108	Coffee tree	41	Gerbera	64
Baby's tears	119	Coleus	120	German violet	56
Bamboo palm	106	Common box	26	Gloxinia	117
Banana plant	86	Creeping fig	61	Good luck palm	32
Bead plant	91	Creeping moss	116	Good luck plant	42
Begonia	23	Crocodile fern	83	Goosefoot plant	124
Bird's nest fern	22	Croton	40	Grape ivy	36
Blushing Bromeliad	88	Ctenanthe	65	Guzmania	66
Boat orchid	49	Cyclamen	48	Hen & chicks	54
Boston fern	90	Cymbidium	49	Houseleek	11
Brake fern	104	Daffodil	87	Hyacinth	72
Bunny ears cactus	93	Date palm	101	Hydrangea	73
Busy Lizzie	75	Delta maidenhair	9	Indian azalea	108
Butterfly orchid	92	Dumb cane	52	Indian shot plant	28
Button fern	96	Dwarf fan palm	33	Ivy	68
Calathea crocata	65	Earth star	45	Ivy tree	57
Calla lily	132	Elephant's ear	14	Jade plant	44
Cape jasmine	63	Elkhorn fern	103	Japanese aralia	58
Cape primrose	123	Emerald fern	19	Japanese azalea	108
Cast iron plant	21	English ivy	68	Java fern	83
Castor oil plant	58	Eternal flame	65	Jerusalem cherry	118
Chain cactus	107	European fan palm	33	Joseph's coat	40
China doll plant	105	False palm	42	Kaffir lily	38
Chinese evergreen	13	Fern arum	131	Kentia palm	32

Index

Common names and synonyms

Ladder fern	104	Pincushion plant	91	Snakeskin	62
Lemon tree	37	Pink jasmine	76	Spider plant	34
Leopold lily	52	Pink quill	129	Spineless Yucca	130
Lady palm	106	Pitcher plant	112	Spleenwort	22
Living stone	78	Plume asparagus	20	Staghorn fern	103
Madagascar jasmine	122	Poinsettia	55	String of hearts	31
Maidenhair fern	9	Polka dot plant	74	String of pearls	46
Maidenhair vine	85	Pot Mum/Mum	35	Stromanthe	65
Malayan coconut palm	39	Prayer plant	81	Sweetheart Hoya	71
Meadow spike moss	116	Prickly pear	93	Sweetheart plant	100
Mind your own business	119	Radiator plant	97	Swiss cheese plant	84
Mini rose	109	Ribbon plant	53	Sword fern	90
Mistletoe cactus	107	Rosary vine	31	Tail flower	17
Money plant	44	Rose grape	82	Ti plant	42
Monkey cups	89	Rose of China	69	*Tillandsia cyanea*	129
Moth orchid	99	Rubber plant	60	Umbrella grass/plant	50
Mother-in-law's tongue	111	Saffron spike	18	Umbrella tree	113
Moulded wax	54	Sago palm	47	Vanda orchid	127
Natal lily	38	Satin pothos	115	Venus fly trap	112
Orange tree	37	Scarlet star	66	Venus slipper orchid	94
Ornamental pineapple	16	*Senecio cruentus*	98	Wax plant	71
Painted leaf Begonia	24	*Senecio rowleyanus*	46	Weeping fig	59
Paper flower	25	Silver crown	43	Winter cherry	118
Paper plant	25	Silver dollar plant	44	Winter jasmine	76
Parlour palm	32	Silver evergreen	13	Wire vine	85
Passion flower	95	Silver ruffles	43	Yucca	130
Patio rose	109	Silver vase plant	10	Zebra cactus	67
Peace lily	121	Silver vine	115	Zebra plant	18
Pearl plant	67	Silver-inch plant	126	ZZ plant	131
Persian violet	56	Singapore orchid	51		
Pickaback plant	125	Slipper flower	27		
Pin wheel	11	Slipper orchid	94		
Pincushion cactus	80	Snake plant	111		

Acknowledgements...
...and thanks

The author would like to gratefully acknowledge the following organisations and sources of reference:
RHS Practical Houseplant Book, Fran Bailey & Zia Allaway
RHS Practical Cactus & Succulent Book, Fran Bailey & Zia Allaway
The Houseplant Expert, Dr. D.G. Hessayon
The Houseplant Survival Manual, William Davidson
100 Great Houseplants, John Evans
Pocket Guide to Orchids, Geoffrey Hands
The Professional Florists' Manual, Lynda Owen
The RHS Gardener's Encyclopedia of Plants and Flowers
Floradania and their excellent image bank and plant database www.floradania.dk
Flower Council of Holland www.flowercouncil.co.uk
RHS Plant Selector rhs.org.uk
Dave's Garden www.davesgarden.com for pronunciation help.

Huge thanks also go out to:
Janet Bowyer at Corner House Design & Print for whom there will never be enough rice cakes to say thank you for all her hard work over and above the call of duty in the design and layout of this book.
Margaret Dunn and Brett Whale for sound suggestions and proof reading.
Jane Benefield DTLLS, MDPF Floristry Course Manager at Moreton Morrell College, Warwickshire for her advice on the selection of houseplants and enthusiasm for the project from start to finish.

This book is dedicated to the memory of my mother & father.

Photography Credits:
Floradania.dk 3, 15, 27-29, 31, 32, 42, 46, 63, 67, 69, 75, 80, 85, 90, 95, 97, 109, 122, 123, Flower Council of Holland 25, 30, M. Follon 30. Following images ©Shutterstock.com. A Little Sihouetto 112, A.Andri 81, AfricaStudi 55, 82, Akarawut 133, A.Wallace 11, FJEA 125, Floki 138, Flower Studio 51, A.Kaminska 86, APalam 45, Arka 38, 39, A. Psom 44, B. Sonjachnyj 137, B Wylezich 41, bjphotograph 35, Chatnara 13, C.Russell 16, Cynoclub 49, 83,127, Davipath 19, D.wski 48, E. Zajchikova 77, Fotogestoeber 87, F. Victoria 71, G. Syngaievsk 110, GLandStudio 60, 62, Gordine 56, Grinton 58, Hvoya 102, Icrm 23, Infoflowersplants 8,43, Insancita 31,138, I.Fisher 66, IURII.B 113, J.Thonguthum 138, J.Sebesta 21, Joloei 94,103, J Deshaie 74, Kamnua 88, K.Denis 137, Moonita 71, K.alexay 53, Kttpugart 20, L. Nishimoto 106, M. Kunz 133, M.Schuppich 118, Madlen 91, M.Lucky 114, MaraZ 79, Melica 119, Memaggiesea 64, Miss S. Teeramat 104,107,128, Moolkum 12, Motorolka 34, 65, 99,102, Nataliass 57, 59, Natalie Studio 98,117, Nattavu 134, Natu 9, New Africa 121, NOPPHARAT STUDIO 969,138, Odua Imag 100, Oksankas 129, Olga 78345,105, Olga P 38, O. Sapegia 124, P. Chan 47, Pegeasen 126, P. Nikonen 22, 111, 130, P.Ksini 73, Peredaniankina 86, Photology1971,14, 53, 84, 131, Phototalker 135, qSPOoKYp 54, R. Hainer 40, R. Lessman 138, S. Elena 36, Sarah2,138, Shooarts 24, Shyya 52, S. Tha 39, Smit 134, Smspsy 72, Spinett 115, S. VanHorn 136, S. Bower 10, Stockpicturegarden 17, 108, 136, 137, Sunny-baby 75, Supapurnkh 50, Susii 68, Taigi, T.Kulikova 92, T. Tortue 96, T. Klejudysz 138, Tunedin 61, 33, V. Telyatnikova 132, Vahe 3D 101, V. Volkov 37, V. Kirdan 138, Vitalinka 120, Vnlit 70, White Maple 78, YeugeniyII 18, Zuzha 26.